Our Changing Population

Series Editor: Cara Acred

Volume 292

Independence Educational Publishers

First published by Independence Educational Publishers

The Studio, High Green

Great Shelford

Cambridge CB22 5EG

England

© Independence 2016

ISBN-13: 9781861687289

Printed in Great Britain
Zenith Print Group

Contents

Introduction

Our Changing Population is Volume 292 in the **ISSUES** series. The aim of the series is to offer current, diverse information about important issues in our world, from a UK perspective.

ABOUT OUR CHANGING POPULATION

Despite population growth rates declining worldwide, by the year 2050 the world's population is predicted to increase from seven billion to nine billion people. This book looks at current population trends across the globe and in the UK. It also looks at issues such as life expectancy, the impact of migration on the UK population and whether we have enough space for our increasing number of residents. Global issues include which countries will see the most population growth, what future cities will look like and whether the Earth can sustain nine billion people.

OUR SOURCES

Titles in the **ISSUES** series are designed to function as educational resource books, providing a balanced overview of a specific subject.

The information in our books is comprised of facts, articles and opinions from many different sources, including:

⇨ Newspaper reports and opinion pieces

⇨ Website factsheets

⇨ Magazine and journal articles

⇨ Statistics and surveys

⇨ Government reports

⇨ Literature from special interest groups

A NOTE ON CRITICAL EVALUATION

Because the information reprinted here is from a number of different sources, readers should bear in mind the origin of the text and whether the source is likely to have a particular bias when presenting information (or when conducting their research). It is hoped that, as you read about the many aspects of the issues explored in this book, you will critically evaluate the information presented.

It is important that you decide whether you are being presented with facts or opinions. Does the writer give a biased or unbiased report? If an opinion is being expressed, do you agree with the writer? Is there potential bias to the 'facts' or statistics behind an article?

ASSIGNMENTS

In the back of this book, you will find a selection of assignments designed to help you engage with the articles you have been reading and to explore your own opinions. Some tasks will take longer than others and there is a mixture of design, writing and research-based activities that you can complete alone or in a group.

FURTHER RESEARCH

At the end of each article we have listed its source and a website that you can visit if you would like to conduct your own research. Please remember to critically evaluate any sources that you consult and consider whether the information you are viewing is accurate and unbiased.

Useful weblinks

www.article13.com

www.channel4.com

www.theconversation.com

www.esrc.ac.uk

www.huffingtonpost.co.uk

www.theguardian.com

www.ibtimes.co.uk

www.migrationobservatory.ox.ac.uk

www.nhs.uk

www.ons.gov.uk

www.populationandsustainability.org/

www.populationmatters.org

www.sustainablefoodtrust.org

www.telegraph.co.uk

www.un.org

Population

The story of our species is one of remarkable success. From a starting point in Africa, our ancestors spread across the planet, harnessing local resources and adapting to the harshest environments.

While some societies collapsed once they had exhausted local resources, and other groups migrated to new lands or fought wars over diminishing local resources, the overall picture was one of continued growth. As technological advances enabled our ancestors to increase agricultural output, their numbers grew exponentially.

The lack of open discussion about this topic means most people are not aware that our high numbers today are such a recent phenomenon. As recently as 1930, in our parents' or grandparents'

youth, world population was some two billion compared with the seven billion living on the planet now.

Current trends

The population trends projected by the UN vary enormously by region:

⇨ Africa and much of Asia are predicted to grow significantly;

⇨ the Americas are expected to grow somewhat; and

⇨ Europe is predicted to stabilise.

The mid-range global projection is that the planet's population will increase from seven billion to nine billion by 2050. Broader estimates range from eight to 11 billion, depending on how effectively and quickly reproductive and development programmes are implemented in developing areas of the world to address the key drivers of population

growth: the lack of reproductive health and contraception, lack of women's rights and poverty. In some countries, migration also contributes significantly to the increase in population.

Population growth rates worldwide are declining but absolute numbers are still rising at one and a half million every week. Growth is also variable; populations are declining in some countries while continuing to grow rapidly in others.

Universal access to reproductive health services is one of the main factors that help to reduce birth rates and hence population growth.

Improvements made to infrastructure, wide availability of modern contraceptives and the empowerment of women all greatly contribute to significantly lower and therefore much more sustainable rates of birth.

Economic development also helps to lift women out of the high birth rate poverty trap.

Across the planet, societies face other population challenges, including ageing and migration.

⇨ The above information is reprinted with kind permission from Population Matters. Please visit www.populationmatters.org for further information.

© Population Matters 2015

Annual mid-year population estimates

Main points

⇨ The population of the UK at 30 June 2014 is estimated to be 64,596,800.

⇨ Over the year to mid-2014 the number of people resident in the UK increased by 491,100 (up 0.77%), which is above the average annual increase (0.75%) seen over the last decade.

⇨ The population increase in the year to mid-2014 included natural growth of 226,200 people (777,400 births minus 551,200 deaths).

⇨ Net international migration of 259,700 people in the year to mid-2014 (582,600 international migrants arrived in the UK and 322,900 migrants left the UK to live abroad) also added to population growth.

⇨ An increase to the population in the year to mid-2014 of 5,200 was due to other changes and adjustments; mainly in the armed forces.

⇨ The number of births occurring in the year to mid-2014 is down on that seen in the previous year (down 1.9%), continuing the downward movement seen in births since the recent peak in the year to mid-2012.

⇨ Net international migration in the year to mid-2014 is the highest since the year to mid-2011 and up by 76,300 from 183,400 last year.

⇨ The median age of the population (the age at which half the population is younger and half the population is older) at mid-2014 was 40 years – the highest ever estimated.

⇨ The number and proportion of older people continues to rise, with over 11.4 million (17.7% of the population) aged 65 and over in mid-2014, up from 11.1 million (17.4%) last year.

The mid-year estimates refer to the population on 30 June of the reference year and are published annually. They are the official set of population estimates for the UK and its constituent countries, the regions and counties of England, and local authorities and their equivalents. This publication relates to the first release of the mid-2014 estimates of the UK and the revised mid-2013 estimates.

The UK mid-year estimates series brings together population estimates that are produced annually for England and Wales by the Office for National Statistics (ONS), for Scotland by National Records of Scotland (NRS) and for Northern Ireland by the Northern Ireland Statistics and Research Agency (NISRA). The timetables for population outputs are available for each country on their respective websites.

The official 2014 mid-year estimates for the UK referred to in this bulletin, build on the mid-2013 estimates, which are updated to account for population change during the period between 1 July 2013 and 30 June 2014 to give the mid-2014 estimates. A combination of registration, survey and administrative data are used to estimate the different components of population change and as such there will be a level of uncertainty associated with the estimated population.

Mid-year population estimates relate to the usually resident population. They account for long-term international migrants (people who change their country of usual residence for a period of 12 months or more) but do not account for short-term migrants (people who come to or leave the country for a period of less than 12 months). This approach is consistent with the standard UN definition for population estimates which is based upon the concept of usual residence and includes people who reside, or intend to reside, in the country for at least 12 months, whatever their nationality.

The mid-year population estimates are essential building blocks for a wide range of National Statistics. They are used directly as a base for other secondary population statistics, such as population projections, population estimates of the very old and population

estimates for small geographical areas. They are used for weighting survey estimates such as the Labour Force Survey and other social surveys to ensure that they are representative of the total population.

The estimates are also used as denominators for rates or ratios, for example in health and economic indicators; the mid-year reference date population estimate for example providing a simple estimate of the "population at risk" for health data collected on a calendar year basis.

The mid-year population estimates are an important input for a wide number of economic and social statistics. Main users include central and local government and the health sector, where they are used for planning and monitoring service delivery, resource allocation and managing the economy. Additionally, they are used by a wider range of organisations such as commercial companies (for market research), special interest groups and academia as well as being of interest to the general public.

What do the mid-2014 UK population estimates show?

This section describes the latest UK population estimates. It shows the latest available estimates for mid-2014 together with the components of population change estimated for the period 1 July 2013 to 30 June 2014.

The population of the UK almost reached 64.6 million in mid-2014 with the total UK population standing at 64,596,800, with a 95% confidence interval of = 0.2%.

Comparing the latest population estimates for mid-2014 with the mid-2013 estimates shows that:

⇨ the population of England increased by 450,800 (up 0.84%) to 54,316,600 accounting for 84% of the UK's population; England's population grew more quickly than any other UK country during the year

⇨ the population of Scotland increased by 19,900 (up 0.37%) to 5,347,600 and accounts for 8% of the UK's population

⇨ the population of Wales increased by 9,600 (up 0.31%) to 3,092,000 and accounts for 5% of the UK's population

⇨ the population of Northern Ireland increased by 10,800 (up 0.59%) to 1,840,500 and accounts for 3% of the UK's population.

How has the UK's population changed?

In the year to mid-2014 the population of the UK increased by 491,100 (up 0.77%).

The increase was driven primarily by net international migration of 259,700 accounting for 53% of the change, followed by natural change (the balance of births minus deaths) of 226,200 accounting for 46% of the change, with other changes of 5,200 making up the remaining increase of 1%.

Compared to the last ten year period, the population change for the year to mid-2014 has some notable features:

⇨ international migration inflow is at its highest since the year to mid-2011, though both international migration inflow and outflow are still below the average for the period

⇨ net migration shows an increase of 76,300 from 183,400 last year, being at its highest since the year to mid-2011 making it above average for the period

⇨ the number of births is down on last year's figure and is slightly below the average for the period

⇨ the number of deaths has fallen since last year, being slightly lower than in the year to mid-2010 and the lowest seen for over 50 years.

In addition to the direct impact of migration on the size of the population, current and past international migration also has indirect effects on the size of the population as it changes the numbers of births and deaths in the UK. For example, statistics on the number of births by the country of birth of the mother show that 197,000 live births (25% of total live births) in the UK in 2013 were to mothers born outside the UK. However, this figure should not be interpreted as an estimate of the indirect effect of migration on the size of the population – it is only one aspect of this. A fuller assessment would consider:

⇨ deaths of people who had migrated to the UK

⇨ births to, and deaths of, people who emigrated from the UK (and who would have given birth, or died, in the UK had they not emigrated)

⇨ how to account for births to, and deaths of, UK-born people who had emigrated and subsequently returned to the UK

⇨ how to account for births to, and deaths of, UK-born people who had parents (or grandparents, etc.) who were themselves immigrants

Additional background information on the UK population, its size, characteristics and the causes of population change is available in the Overview of the UK Population.

How has the population changed across the UK?

Population growth in the year to mid-2014 was greatest in southern and eastern England. London had the highest population growth, with population up 1.45%. The East and South East regions of England increased by 1.08% and 0.92%, respectively.

The lowest regional population increases in the year were seen in Wales, North East of England and Scotland growing by 0.31%, 0.32% and 0.37%, respectively. The population of Northern Ireland grew by 0.59%. No country of the UK or region of England experienced a population decrease.

The Officer for National Statistics produces population estimates for other geographies such as parliamentary constituencies, national parks, wards, and health areas for England and Wales. Population estimates for subnational population estimates in Scotland are produced by NRS, and NISRA produces subnational population estimates for Northern Ireland.

London had the largest natural change of all regions with 82,400 more births than deaths; the North East of England and Wales both had the lowest natural change, each with just 3,300 more births than deaths.

London was the destination of more than a third of international migrants arriving in the UK – contributing to it having the highest net international migration of all regions at 107,400 – up by 27,900 from last year; Northern Ireland had the lowest net international migration with 2,200 more people arriving to stay from abroad than emigrating.

The South West of England received more people from other parts of the UK than any other region leading to a 25,700 population increase; and London continued its pattern of having the greatest outflow of people to other parts of the UK of

any region, with a net loss of more than 68,600 people. More people of every age left London for other parts of the UK than arrived, except for people aged 21–28, more of whom arrived in London from other parts of the UK than left.

Approximately two-thirds (64%) of the people moving out of London went to the South East and East of England, a similar picture to last year.

The latest information on internal migration is available in the *2014 Internal Migration by Local Authorities in England and Wales* release.

What are the key population stories at a local level?

There are presently 391 local authorities in the UK; 326 in England, 32 in Scotland, 22 in Wales and 11 in Northern Ireland. In mid-2014, the local authority with the smallest population size at 2,300 was Isles of Scilly and the largest population at 1,101,400 was Birmingham.

The total population grew in 357 local authorities in the year to mid-2014. In total, 13 local authorities had growth of more than 2% in their population.

All of the local authorities with the greatest percentage growth in population in the year to mid-2014 are in England; six of these areas are London boroughs. Growth in these local authorities in the year to mid-2014 was generally due to net international migration, with high rates of natural change - (births minus deaths) in Hackney and an increase in the number of armed forces in Forest Heath. The greatest percentage growth in population in Scotland was 1.8% in Midlothian (ranked 20th); in Wales it was 0.7% in Cardiff (ranked 175th); and in Northern Ireland it was 1.3% in Lisburn and Castlereagh (ranked 53rd).

The total population fell in just 34 local authorities in the year to mid-2014; only Richmondshire had a fall of more than 1% in their population.

The local authorities with the greatest percentage fall in population in the year to mid-2014 are spread across England, Scotland and Wales. No local authority in Northern Ireland had a fall in population in the year to mid-2014.

Population falls in these local authorities were generally due to outflow of people due to internal migration to somewhere else in the UK and negative natural change (more deaths than births). The fall in Richmondshire can be attributed to a sizeable outflow of armed forces personnel during the year to mid-2014, whilst the greatest contributor to the population fall in Harrogate was emigration overseas.

25 June 2015

⇨ The above information is reprinted with kind permission from the Office for National Statistics. Please visit www.ons.gov.uk for further information.

Overview of the UK population

November 2015 release.

How many people are there in the UK and how does this change over time?

The UK population grew to an estimated 64.6 million in 2014, its highest ever value. This represents an increase of almost half a million people from 2013 according to the most recent population estimates. Please note that the population statistics used in this story are mid-year estimates unless otherwise stated.

Population projections are also available which show how the population would change in future years if recent demographic trends were to continue.

UK population estimates and annual growth rates, 1960s to 2020s

Following the relatively high growth in the UK population during the 1960s (the annual growth rate was 0.61% of the UK population), a result of the 1960s' baby boom, population growth slowed during the 1970s and the UK population actually fell between 1975 and 1978. In the 1980s, the UK population grew again (with the exception of 1982 when it fell by 0.12%, its biggest fall since 1951) reaching annual growth of between 0.2% and 0.3% in the latter half of the decade when the 1960s' baby boomers were having children. The 1990s had a stable level of growth, similar to that of the late 1980s.

The annual growth for the UK population more than doubled during the 2000s, from 0.34% in 2000 to 0.71% in 2009; the annual growth rate for the decade more than doubled as well, up from 0.28% in the 1990s to 0.64% in the 2000s. Uplifts in population growth have generally coincided with an increase in the number of countries holding EU membership. Growth in the UK population since 2010 has been similar to that of the late 2000s and while it is projected to be the decade with the biggest period of growth in the last 50 years, UK population growth is then projected to slow steadily, with the long-term annual growth rate projected to stabilise at around 0.3% of the UK population.

How does the UK population compare with other countries?

The UK population is one of the largest in the European Union.

Population Estimates and Annual Growth for Selected EU and non-EU Countries, 2013–2014

The UK population had the third largest population in the EU in 2014: 16.4 million fewer people than Germany and 1.5 million fewer people than France in 2014. The UK had 3.6 million people more than Italy which was the country with the fourth highest population in the EU in 2014. Outside of the EU, Russia had the highest European population, with 143.7 million people in 2014, almost twice the population of Germany. Turkey had the third highest European population, with 76.7 million people in 2014, 12.3 million more people than lived in the UK.

Between 2013 and 2014, the UK population grew faster than that of the EU as a whole: 0.7% growth for the UK population compared with 0.35% growth for the EU. The growth rate for the population of the UK was more than twice that of Ireland, the population for which grew by 0.31% between 2013 and 2014.

Of the 28 countries in the EU, there were four countries where the population grew faster than the UK between 2013 and 2014: Luxembourg, Italy, Malta and Sweden.

There were 13 EU countries where the population shrank between 2013 and 2014; these countries included Poland, Bulgaria, Hungary, Romania, Spain, Portugal and Greece.

What caused the UK population to change?

There are four ways that the UK population changes: people are born, they die, they move in or they move out.

Natural change

Natural change is the number of births minus the number of deaths. Natural change has resulted in increases in the population in every year over the last decade, by around 200,000 people per year on average over the previous decade and in 2014 it increased the UK population by more than 200,000 people.

The number of births per year in the UK was high (above 850,000) from the mid-1950s up until the early 1970s: the 1960s' baby boom. The number of births fell markedly during the 1970s, before rising again in the 1980s and early 1990s, when the 1960s' baby boomers were likely to have children. The number of births peaked again in 2012 when the number of births in the UK was at its highest for 40 years: 813,000 in 2012 compared with 834,000 in 1972.

The number of deaths was more stable than the number of births. From 1953 the number of deaths rose to a peak in 1976 (680,800): when the highest number of deaths since 1918 (715,200) was recorded; and then fell away. The number of UK recorded deaths fell faster in the 2000s than in the previous two decades, falling below 600,000 for the first time since the 1950s, in 2004. Since 2004, the number of UK recorded deaths has remained below 600,000 because people are living longer.

Net migration

Net migration is the number of immigrants minus the number of emigrants. The growth of the UK population since the 1990s has been attributed primarily to the growth of net migration. Net migration has increased the UK population by more than 240,000 people per year on average from 2004 to 2014, which is about 40,000 more people per year than natural change.

Immigration has been higher than emigration since the early 1990s. In the late 1990s, the level of net migration increased from the tens of thousands to the hundreds of thousands. Rises in immigration have tended to coincide with expansion of the European Union allowing more people to freely migrate to the UK. The rise in net migration in 1998 can in part be attributed to instability in countries in Africa, Eastern Europe and the Middle East. International immigration by students increased during the late 2000s, peaking between 2009 and 2011.

In addition to the direct impact of net migration on the size of the population, current and past international migration also has indirect effects on the size and structure of the population as migrants tend to arrive as young adults aged in their 20s to early 40s and they change the numbers of births and deaths in the UK. For example, statistics on the number of births by the country of birth of the mother show that 197,000 live births (25% of total live births) in the UK in 2013 were to mothers born outside the UK. However, this figure should not be interpreted as an estimate of the indirect effect of migration on the size of the population; it is only one aspect of this. A fuller assessment would consider:

⇨ UK born children fathered by men born outside the UK

⇨ deaths of people who had migrated to the UK

⇨ births to, and deaths of, people who emigrated from the UK (and who would have given birth, or died, in the UK had they not emigrated)

⇨ how to account for births to, and deaths of, UK-born people who had emigrated and subsequently returned to the UK

⇨ how to account for births to, and deaths of, UK-born people who had parents (or grandparents, etc.) who were themselves immigrants.

How does the population differ across the UK?

Having seen that the UK population can vary by age and sex, attention now turns to how the UK population differs by country and by region of England.

In 2014 the national and regional populations are not equal in size. Furthermore the number of people per square kilometre (also known as population density) is also very different, with just 69 people per square kilometre in Scotland compared with 5,432 people per square kilometre in London. The population density of London was more than 10 times that of any other region or country.

Population density varies within England, it will also vary within other countries and within the regions of

England: for example in Scotland, Glasgow and Edinburgh will have a larger population density than areas of the Highlands.

The UK 2014 sex ratio was 96.9 males per 100 females. This varies from 94.4 males per 100 females in Scotland to 98.4 males per 100 females in London.

The 2004 to 2014 annual growth rate varied from 0.3% of the regional population in the North East to 1.4% of the regional population in London. The 2004 to 2014 annual growth rate in London was 0.51 percentage points more than for the East of England which had the second highest annual growth rate over the period 2004 to 2014. High population growth in London may be due to its popularity as a destination for graduates and as an initial port of call for many immigrating to the UK.

UK average household size in 2014 was 2.42 people per household. This was broadly similar across the regions, ranging from 2.22 people per household in Scotland to 2.65 people per household in London.

UK life expectancy at birth for 2011 to 2013 was 78.9 years for boys and 82.7 years for girls, a difference of 3.8 years. Male life expectancy varied from 76.8 years in Scotland to 80.4 years in the South East, a range of 3.6 years across the regions and countries of the UK. Female life expectancy ranged from 80.9 years in Scotland to 84.1 years in London, a difference of 3.2 years. The difference between male and female life expectancy varied from 3.5 years in the East of England and the South East to 4.3 years in Northern Ireland; the difference for the UK was 3.8 years.

5 November 2015

⇨ The above information is reprinted with kind permission from the Office for National Statistics. Please visit www.ons.gov.uk for further information.

Britain's population fastest-growing in the EU

The UK has experienced the largest population growth in all of the EU, according to a new report.

By Zairah Khurshid

Britain's population has grown by 6.4 people per 1,000 in the last year to a total 64.8 million people, a report by European Union's statistics agency, Eurostat.Migration is the main factor as to why Britain's population has grown the fastest than any other major European country in the last year.

Germany and France are the only two EU countries with bigger populations than the UK's, but they had lower growth rates at five and 4.5 per 1,000.

"Britain's population has grown by 6.4 people per 1,000 in the last year to a total 64.8 million people"

Luxembourg experienced the largest rise (23.9 people per 1,000), though smaller populations are skewed by sudden surges in arrivals, and recorded larger changes in the rate of population rise. Countries suffering severe economic problems saw their populations fall. Greece, which lost more than eight people in every 1,000 person, and Spain, which lost 1.6 per 1,000 people.

Eurostat said that the population of the EU has risen to 508.2 million at the end of last year, from 507 million from 2013. They also report that 80% of this increase was due to people migrating to the continent, whereas 20% was due to natural growth (the difference between births and deaths).

Britain accepted more asylum seekers last year than 17 other EU countries put together, reported by Eurostat in May. Britain granted asylum protection to 14,065 people in 2014, while other large European states accepted just a few hundred each.

Eritrea, Pakistan, Syria, Iran and Albania were the top countries to apply for asylum in the UK.

Germany remains the most populated EU state, housing 16% of the total EU population. France comes second (13.1%), followed by the UK (12.9%), Italy (12%), Spain (9.1%) and Poland (7.5%).

The Government reports that 159 competitors, spectators or visitors that came to the London Olympics in 2012 and the Commonwealth Games in Glasgow last year have claimed asylum.

Philip Davies, the Conservative MP who obtained the figures in parliament, told *The Daily Telegraph*: "I am very concerned that we are being treated as a soft touch when it comes to asylum."

11 July 2015

⇨ The above information is reprinted with kind permission from *IBTimes*. Please visit www.ibtimes.co.uk for further information.

The impact of migration on population growth

More than half (54%) of the increase of the UK population between 1991 and 2012 was due to the direct contribution of net migration.

The total net inflow of post-2012 migrants accounts for 43% of total population growth until 2037.

The contribution of net migration to population change differs across the four UK constituent nations. Without net immigration, Scotland's population would stagnate over the next two decades and decrease in the longer term.

Net migration assumptions have been continually revised in the projections released since the mid-1990s, reflecting rising levels of net migration and the high uncertainty of migration forecasting.

The reduction in net migration levels in the latest projections does not result in significant slowdown of future population growth from increase of fertility and life expectancy.

Source: The Migration Observatory at the University of Oxford

UK life expectancy expected to rise to late 80s by 2030

"Life expectancy is rising faster than thought, with 90 expected to become the norm in some affluent areas of the country by 2030," *The Guardian* reports. The same predictions led the *Daily Mail* to warn of a "life expectancy timebomb".

A new modelling study looking at trends in life expectancy estimated that male babies born in 2030 could live to an average of 85.7 years, with females living an average of 87.6 years.

The study also flagged up the potential effects of health and socioeconomic inequalities on life expectancy. For example, it estimated life expectancy in the affluent London borough of Kensington and Chelsea would be five to six years higher than the working-class area of Tower Hamlets.

It remains to be seen if the increase in life expectancy would be a blessing or a burden. Elderly people contribute to society in many meaningful ways, such as helping out with childcare or volunteering for charity work. But they may also have complex health needs that could require significant resources to treat.

Assuming the model is accurate, the study produces some interesting results about trends in life expectancy and inequalities, and how they may change over time.

Where did the story come from?

The study was carried out by researchers from the department of epidemiology and biostatistics at the School of Public Health and MRC-PHE Centre for Environment and Health, the UK Small Area Health Statistics Unit, Imperial College London, Northumbria University, and GlaxoSmithKline.

It was funded by the UK Medical Research Council and Public Health England.

The study was published in the peer-reviewed medical journal, *The Lancet*. It has been made available on an open-access basis, so it is free to read online.

Most of the media reported the results of the research well, although they did not question the accuracy of the predictions much. Different outlets focused on different aspects of the research.

The Daily Telegraph and the *Mail* focused on the headline figure that the study predicted higher life expectancies than official estimates. In its headline, the *Telegraph* claimed people would live "up to four years longer" than official estimates, although the study shows a difference of 2.4 years for men and one year for women.

BBC News highlighted the narrowing gap between men and women's life expectancies, while *The Guardian* and *The Independent* were more concerned with the widening gap between rich and poor.

What kind of research was this?

This modelling study analysed death rates and population data for 375 districts of England and Wales. Researchers used the data to construct mathematical models to predict life expectancy from 1981 to 2030 for each of the districts, looking at men and women separately.

The study aimed to give reliable district-level information about life expectancy to help with future planning for health, social service and pension needs. The figures are all averages for the districts and cannot be used to predict individual lifespans.

What did the research involve?

Researchers looked at records of deaths in England and Wales between 1981 and 2012 by local authority district. They combined this with population data to develop five statistical models that could predict future death rates and life expectancy.

The researchers tested the models to see which best predicted actual death rates during the last ten years of the data, then used the best-performing model to predict future life expectancy at the local and national level.

The data in the study came from the Office for National Statistics. The models incorporated features of death rates in relation to people's age, trends of death rates in people who were born within or close to the same five-year period, changes to death rates over time, and by local area.

The test of the five models found one model, which gave greater importance to trends in those born within adjacent time periods, worked better than the others, with forecast errors of 0.01 years for men and women.

This model was best able to predict death rates for 2002–12 using the first 21 years of the data. The researchers therefore chose this model to predict life expectancy from 2012–30.

While the geographical areas of the districts remained the same over the study, people living in these areas obviously change. The researchers looked at trends for each district, including birth rates and migration, so they could factor this in.

They looked at how relative levels of deprivation for each district affected the mortality rates and life expectancy. Taking account of all this data, they then predicted how life expectancy at birth could change from babies born in 2012 to babies born in 2030.

Rates for men and women were calculated separately, as life expectancy differs by gender. As far as we can tell from the paper, the analysis was done using reasonable assumptions about population trends.

What were the basic results?

The study found life expectancy in England and Wales is expected to continue to rise from the 2012 average of 79.5 years for men and 83.3 for women, to 85.7 (95% credible interval 84.2 to 87.4) for men and 87.6 (95% credible interval 86.7 to 88.9) for women by 2030.

This is higher than predictions from the Office of National Statistics. However, this will come at the cost of increasing inequality between districts.

Improvements in life expectancy from 1981–2012 varied a great deal between districts. In 1981, men in districts with the best life expectancies could expect to live 5.2 years longer than those in the areas with the lowest life expectancies (4.5 for women).

By 2012, this had increased to a difference of 6.1 years for men and 5.6 years for women. The study says this trend is expected to accelerate, so that by 2030 the difference in life expectancy between the best and worst districts could reach 8.3 years for both men and women.

Most of the districts with the lowest life expectancies now and in 2030 were in south Wales and the northeast and northwest of England. The areas with the highest life expectancy were mostly in the south of England and London. However, London districts varied from the highest to the lowest life expectancy levels.

The gap between men and women's life expectancy is expected to shrink further. It has already shrunk from six years in 1981 to 3.8 years in 2012, and by 2030 it could be only 1.9 years. In some areas, there may be no difference between men and women's life expectancy at all.

How did the researchers interpret the results?

The researchers say their results are a more accurate prediction of how life expectancy will increase than official figures, and are the first to look consistently at changes in life expectancy at the district level over a long period of time.

They say the increase is likely to be the result of better survival in people over the age of 65. They say men's life expectancy will rise faster than women's, partly because of the effect of social trends such as smoking among middle-aged and older women.

The researchers claim the data will allow local authorities to plan better for the future, especially as much health and social care is now the responsibility of local areas. However, they also say the figures provide a warning that inequality in England and Wales will continue to rise.

Conclusion

This analysis of population data provides some fascinating information about how life expectancy has changed over the past 30 years, and how it may change in the future.

It found life expectancy for men and women will continue to rise. However, it also found the existing trends of the difference in life expectancy between different districts will continue to rise, which is of concern.

Although the data shows more deprived areas have seen less of an improvement in life expectancy, the study cannot inform us what factors are responsible for the differences in life expectancy.

There is one big limitation of any study that predicts life expectancy in the future: the figures are always based on trends from death rates in the past, and assume that past trends will continue into the future.

These types of studies cannot account for unexpected events or major social changes that could have a huge effect on life expectancy. For example, they can't build into their models the potential for unlikely events such as a big natural disaster, changes within the healthcare system, or even a major health breakthrough, such as a cure for heart disease or cancer.

It's worth remembering, too, that life expectancy figures represent the life expectancy of a baby born in that particular year. So the life expectancy figures for 2012 don't represent life expectancy for adults alive in 2012, but for babies born that year. This means the figures for 2030 don't yet apply: they are only predictions for babies born in the future.

The study can't be used by individuals to predict how long they may live, but it does provide useful data to plan for pensions and health and social provisions in the future.

If you are keen to live to 2030 and beyond, your best bet is to take steps to reduce your risk of the five leading causes of premature death:

⇨ cancer

⇨ heart disease

⇨ stroke

⇨ respiratory disease

⇨ liver disease.

30 April 2015

⇨ The above information is reprinted with kind permission from NHS Choices. Please visit www.nhs.uk for further information.

© NHS Choices 2015

The UK, the world and the people

Information from the ESRC about World Population Day 2014.

The world's population has reached 7.2 billion and counting – literally, if you take a look at this world population clock. By 2025, world population could be more than eight billion people. Around 2047 it could hit nine billion and by 2100 it could reach 11 billion – although there is still much uncertainty around this number with some estimates reaching 16 billion.

"The World Population Day theme for 2014 was 'Investing in young people' – a topic of universal importance, but especially relevant for developing countries," says Dr Jakub Bijak of the ESRC Centre for Population Change. He is an expert on social statistics and demography at the University of Southampton.

The under-15s comprise more than a quarter of the global population, Dr Bijak points out.

"The world today has its largest generation of youth in history – 1.8 billion young people, mostly in developing countries – with enormous potential to help tackle the major challenges facing humanity," says UN Secretary-General Ban Ki-moon in a statement for World Population Day.

But looking specifically at the UK population, what does the future hold? The overall population is set to reach 73 million people by 2037, according to the Office for National Statistics. Some 57 per cent of the projected increase is set to be driven by 'projected natural increase', which essentially means more births than deaths – while the remaining 43 per cent is down to net migration (those arriving minus those leaving).

One thing which can be said with some certainty is that the UK will be more ethnically diverse, says Dr Bijak. He cites ethnic population projections from the ESRC-funded UPTAP programme (Understanding Population Trends and Processes), which finished in 2010.

But while the future UK population likely will continue to grow – mainly due to more births than deaths – future migration levels are actually more uncertain.

"Even though in the last two years net migration was relatively stable, we do not know whether this will continue," says Dr Bijak. "Besides, estimates of migration to and from the UK are based on a sample survey, which bears large random errors, so an apparent increase or decrease in migration estimates may not be significant in a statistical sense.

"This is why demographers try to move from trying to predict the future population exactly, which is not possible, to describing the uncertainty – the likelihood of different possible outcomes – which can be then taken into account in planning and policymaking."

"As for Europe – and indeed the rest of the world – the main issue is that different countries are really diverse when it comes to future population change," he adds.

In several European countries, the birth rate is declining. Many Western European countries, including Spain, Italy and Germany have total fertility rates below 2.1 births per woman – the rate they would need to achieve to keep population at the same level.

Birth rates aside, the UK is among EU countries with the largest inflows of foreign nationals, but it's not unique, according to figures in the House of Commons library. In 2011, the UK came second among the EU countries with an inflow of 418,000 foreign nationals, and ranked third in net migration with 239,000.

But the big picture in terms of population growth remains the developing world, Dr Bijak emphasises. The highest growth occurs in poor countries – and the countries with the fastest growth rates already have difficulties feeding their populations.

11 July 2014

⇨ The above information is reprinted with kind permission from the ESRC. Please visit www.esrc.ac.uk for further information.

The impact of migration on UK population growth

Based on official population estimates and population projections, this briefing examines the impact of migration on recent and future UK demographic trends.

Key points

⇨ More than half (54%) of the increase of the UK population between 1991 and 2012 was due to the direct contribution of net migration.

⇨ Differences in net migration assumptions between the 'low' and the 'high' variant projections produce a range of variation of 3.3 million in the projected size of the UK population in 2037 (between 71.6 and 75.0 million).

⇨ In the principal projection the cumulative net inflow of post-2012 migrants accounts for 43% of total population growth until 2037. A further 17% of projected population growth is attributable to the additional contribution of new migrants to natural change (i.e. births and deaths).

⇨ The projected contribution of net migration to population change considerably differs across the four UK constituent nations. Without net immigration, Scotland's population would stagnate over the next two decades and decrease in the longer term.

⇨ Net migration assumptions have been continually revised in the projections released since the mid-1990s, reflecting rising levels of net migration and the high uncertainty of migration forecasting. The reduction in assumed net migration levels in the latest projections (relative to the previous 2010-based release) does not result in significant slowdown of future population growth because of the concurrent projected increase of fertility and life expectancy.

Net migration exceeded natural change for a decade

Population estimates show that net migration was a major component of population growth over the past two decades.

In particular, annual net migration has substantially increased since the beginning of the 1990s, exceeding natural change as a driver of UK demographic trends in all years from mid-1998 to mid-2011. However, natural change has remained positive throughout the last two decades and has also continually increased from 2001 onwards, in particular due to a rise in the number of births. As a result of a significant drop of net migration (by almost 100,000), 2011–12 was the first year in more than a decade when natural change contributed more to the growth of the UK population than net migration. Overall, between mid-1991 and mid-2012 net migration (resulting in an addition of 3.4 million people to the UK population) accounted for just over half (54%) of UK population growth.

However, this retrospective analysis does not account for the contribution of past migration to natural change – mainly to births, given that migrants are mostly young, healthy individuals. The number of births over a given period is determined both by the size and age structure of the female population and by fertility rates (i.e. the average number of children per woman in each age group). Migration impacts on both factors – i.e. it affects the number of women of childbearing age and, if migrant women have different fertility patterns, the total fertility rate of the population as a whole. A recent ONS report (Dormon 2014) using

the latest Census data for England and Wales has shown that births to foreign-born women made up 25.5% of all births in 2011, up from 16.4% one decade earlier (2001). For a shorter period (2001–07) and for the UK as a whole, Tromans et al. (2009) estimated the overall contribution of foreign-born women to the increase in number of births at 65%. However, this was mainly due to the increase in the number of foreign-born women of childbearing age – total fertility rates of non-UK born women remained constant between 2001 and 2011 (2.21 in both years), resulting in a decreasing gap with the fertility levels of UK-born women that increased from 1.56 to 1.84 over the same period (Dormon 2014). While these figures certainly point to the significant indirect contribution that immigration is making to UK population trends, it has to be noted that this analysis, by referring to country of birth: (a) considers a temporally broad definition of the migrant population (i.e. the overall impact on births of in-migration over the past three or more decades, not only the contribution of those who moved to the UK during the observed period) and (b) does not single out the effect of emigration (of both UK- and foreign-born women) and of immigration of UK-born women.

UK population projected to grow to 71–75 million by 2037

The projected size of the UK population in the period to 2037, including high migration, low migration, 'balanced' net migration and zero net migration variants of the 2012-based projections.

In the principal projection of net migration at +165,000 per year, the size of the UK population is projected to increase by almost ten million between 2012 and 2037 – from 63.7 million to 73.3 million, an increase of 15%. In this demographic scenario, the UK population will reach 70 million in 2027. The different net migration levels assumed in the high migration and low migration variants (±60,000 per year) lead to a variation after 25 years of ±1.7 million people – or, in relative terms, a 5% difference between the low migration and high migration variant. Projected population size in 2037 according to the long-term 'balanced' net migration variant (which assumes convergence of net migration to zero towards the end of the projection) is only marginally lower (-0.5 million) than in the low migration variant. In the zero migration variant, the projected population size reaches 67.5 million in 2037, or 7.9% less than the principal projection.

Net migration accounts for over two-thirds of projected population growth

The UK population is projected to rise both because of positive natural change and because of positive net migration. Population growth in the absence of further migration would total 3.8 million, equivalent to 39.4% of the total increase in the principal projection. However, the size of the UK population with no additional net migration would level off at 67.5 million over the next three decades and would eventually decline if the projections are carried forward beyond mid-century. In the principal projection the cumulative net inflow of new migrants accounts for 43.5% of total population growth, i.e. an addition of 4.2 million. The additional (indirect) contribution of post-2012 immigrants to natural change until 2037 is estimated at 1.6 million, i.e. 17.1% of projected population growth. In total, therefore, 60.6% of the expected increase in the UK population is attributable, directly or indirectly, to future net migration. It should also be emphasised that, while these calculations are based on the same assumptions about future fertility and mortality rates irrespective of the assumed level of net migration, fertility and mortality rates for recent migrants are likely to differ, to some extent, from those for the long-established population – e.g. assuming higher fertility rates for post-2012 immigrant women would imply a larger indirect contribution of migration to natural change.

References

Dormon O. "Childbearing of UK and non-UK born women living in the UK - 2011 Census data." ONS, London, February 2014.

Herm A. and M. Poulain. "International Migration Data as Input for Population Projections." Working Paper 20, Joint Eurostat/UNECE Work Session on Demographic Projections, Lisbon, 28-30 April 2010.

ONS. "Methodology Guide for Mid-2011 Population Estimates, England and Wales." ONS, London, 2012.

ONS. "Revised Annual Mid-year Population Estimates, 2001 to 2010." ONS, London, December 2013.

ONS. "Background and methodology: 2012-based national population projections." ONS, London, November 2013.

Tromans N, E. Natamba, and J. Jefferies. "Have Women Born outside the UK Driven the Rise in UK Births since 2001?" Population Trends 136 (2009):28-42.

19 February 2014

⇨ The above information is reprinted with kind permission from The Migration Observatory. Please visit www.migrationobservatory.ox.ac.uk for further information.

Britain is not ready for the coming population boom

Our bulging kingdom will soon hold 70 million people, but there is no certainty that its government has a plan for their welfare.

By Telegraph View

In 1996, when the population of England was 49 million, it was projected to be around 51 million today. The latest figures from the Office for National Statistics show that it now stands at just over 54 million.

We are seeing the fastest growth in population since the post-war baby boom, when a high birth rate was something to be encouraged, since countries whose populations stagnate and decline have a bleak future. Historically, a rising population meant more people available to work – and a bigger economy brought greater wealth. But the drivers of the current rise are different from those of the past.

"We are seeing the fastest growth in population since the post-war baby boom, when a high birth rate was something to be encouraged"

The principal motor is immigration, both directly through new arrivals and indirectly through a higher birth rate among younger settlers. A secondary cause is longevity. The median age (at which half the population is younger and half older) is now 40, the highest ever.

The problem with the inaccuracy of past demographic forecasts is that little or no preparation was made for a population of the size it is now. This is essentially a problem for England – which is one of the most densely populated large countries in the world – and particularly for London and the South East, where most of the growth has occurred. The pressure on transport infrastructure, education, healthcare and other services is apparent to anyone who lives or works there.

On current trends the population for the UK will reach 70 million in 2027. Over a period of 20 years it will have risen by the same amount it increased in the previous 60. Unless this is going to be stopped, and it is hard to see how it will be, then it is incumbent on the Government to provide the schools, roads and hospitals to cope with the numbers. Recent experience of Westminster's capacity for long-term planning does not leave much room for encouragement.

25 June 2015

⇨ The above information is reprinted with kind permission from *The Telegraph*. Please visit www. telegraph.co.uk for further information.

There's plenty more space for humanity on this 'tiny' island

Reports of our booming population are predictably being used to spout bigotry on immigration. A lack of room is the least of Britain's problems.

By Zoe Williams

By 2039, the Office for National Statistics expects the UK population to be 74.3 million, an increase that is accounted for, in almost exactly equal parts, by immigration and natural growth (more births than deaths). Its estimates of net migration are 256,000 next year, 232,000 the year after, dropping below 200,000 in the 2020s. Given that net migration was over 300,000 last year, and the average over the past decade has been 250,000, the real story here is that the ONS expects migration to decrease. At a guess that'll be because, by 2020, word will have got out to the world that our public services have been asset-stripped and we're all slogging through a low-wage, high-rent economy in a state of neo-Georgian servitude.

The ONS has said two things, in other words: first, that migration is expected to go down; second, that population trends half-spring from the invigorating human propensity to cling to life, and create life, wherever it

can. And these messages have been ignored or turned on their heads to become, this TINY island is being SWAMPED by foreigners.

Upon this false premise is built an entire cathedral of nonsense. Nowhere, not even in the debate about renewable energy, is misinformation distributed so liberally and shamelessly by reputable people, MPs and commentators, who don't even have the excuse of illiteracy.

There is no shortage of space on this island. It may be tiny, especially when you place it atop Sweden, and it may seem improbable, trying to visually conceive its geographical limits, that 74 million people could squash themselves on to it. But there's really no need for that bogus exercise, when perfectly good data exists on how much of the UK is urbanised – 10.6% of England, 1.9% of Scotland, 3.6% of Northern Ireland and 4.1% of Wales. When you add in parks, gardens and other open spaces

within the built environment, the proportion of 'developed' England drops to 2.3%. There may be too many of us for the things we can be bothered to build – houses, schools, hospitals – but there are not too many of us for the space that we have, nor will there be in 2025.

This isn't an argument for unbridled development, and nor does it intend to minimise how much overcrowding there is, when we all try to live in the same bit of that 2.3%. People cannot simply be sent to build shacks in Wales, when they overspill from Bristol. Most of the natural world needs to be left unmolested if we're to have any quality of life.

Nevertheless, the potential here is vast – were productive industry nurtured, developed but underpopulated areas would have jobs for people to move for. Were development undertaken systematically and with a social purpose, rather than up-against-a-wall and on the cheap, population growth could be welcomed rather than dreaded.

Which brings us to housing. We have a housing crisis on one hand, and high immigration on the other, and those two facts are always left hanging since the causal link between them is apparently so obvious. The fact is, they are not related: house building is slack, but the supply of rooms per person has never been higher; what has really changed is who owns what and who can afford to rent it from them. Plainly, if there were visionary local councils throwing up plentiful, mixed-tenure developments, that would alter the picture somewhat, but what we're really looking at is a rentier power dynamic. Capital holds all the cards in housing, and is concentrated in very few hands. A world without migration wouldn't alter that.

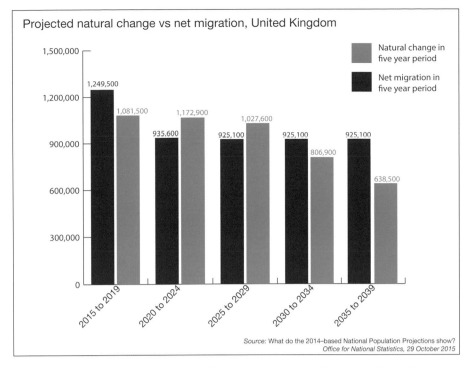

Projected natural change vs net migration, United Kingdom

Legend:
- Natural change in five year period (grey)
- Net migration in five year period (black)

Values:
- 2015 to 2019: 1,249,500 (net migration), 1,081,500 (natural change)
- 2020 to 2024: 935,600 (net migration), 1,172,900 (natural change)
- 2025 to 2029: 925,100 (net migration), 1,027,600 (natural change)
- 2030 to 2034: 925,100 (net migration), 806,900 (natural change)
- 2035 to 2039: 925,100 (net migration), 638,500 (natural change)

Source: What do the 2014–based National Population Projections show?
Office for National Statistics, 29 October 2015

Low wages, likewise, are laid at the feet of recent arrivals. The fault line here is between those who argue that, while immigrants may slightly bring down wages sectorially, their boost to GDP makes up for it, and those who counter that it doesn't feel that way to the people working in the affected sectors. This is an infuriating diversion: the people to blame for low wages are the people who pay low wages. The sectors crammed with workers not earning a living wage (this, according to the Living Wage Foundation at the weekend, amounts to six million people) have spent decades whittling down pay. Migrant labour is merely one tool in their kit. The key victory has been the propaganda push that has reclassified low-paid work as 'low-skilled' to justify harvesting most of its output as profit.

Immigrants have been successfully, egregiously framed as a threat. All sources of immigration have become one. The debate refuses to distinguish between a student and an engineer and a cockle picker and a refugee. Never mind that our universities are a major export, and without foreign students our balance of payments would be stuffed; never mind that sharing expertise across borders is what allows creativity and innovation to flourish; never mind that the exploitation of workers is a case for employers to answer, and it is not for the exploited to apologise for being too plentiful; never mind that we are signatories of the refugee convention and were, in living memory, proud of that fact. The result is that we will now stand by and watch people freeze and, in some cases, literally rot in makeshift European camps, because they're probably 'economic' migrants, and even though we know they're not, we can't have them because they take up space and we're too tiny.

The deliberate lack of sophistication has led, inexorably, to a lack of humanity, sitting on the terrain like a toxic fog, choking any pride we could reasonably take in our national character. Those purporting to protect Britain from the outside threat of the stranger are actually destroying its values from within.

1 November 2015

⇨ The above information is reprinted with kind permission from *The Guardian*. Please visit www.theguardian.com for further information.

What is a long-term international migrant?

A long-term international migrant is defined as someone who moves to a country other than that of his or her usual residence for a period of at least a year, so that the country of destination becomes his or her new country of usual residence.

What is net migration?

Net migration is the difference between people moving into the UK (immigration) and people moving out of the UK (emigration). If net migration is positive then it means that more people have moved to live in the UK than have left to live elsewhere.

The latest headline figures

Our latest provisional estimates of Long Term International Migration (LTIM) show that net migration stood at 336,000 in the year ending June 2015. This is up from 254,000 in the year ending June 2014. This is a statistically significant increase.

636,000 people immigrated to the UK in the year ending June 2015, a statistically significant increase compared with 574,000 in the previous year. Emigration was stable with 300,000 people leaving the UK in the year ending June 2015 compared with 320,000 in the previous year.

Source: *Net migration to the UK was estimated to be 336,000 in the year ending June 2015, Office for National Statistics, 26 November 2015*

Concise Report on the World Population Situation in 2014

An extract from **The World Population Situation in 2014: A Concise Report** *by the* **United Nations.**

Introduction

The present report provides a demographic perspective on how the world has changed over the past 20 years. The world has witnessed many profound social, economic and political changes since the International Conference on Population and Development, held in Cairo in 1994. Few factors will shape the future global development agenda as fundamentally as the size, structure and spatial distribution of the world's population. Ongoing demographic transitions associated with changing levels and patterns of fertility, mortality and migration continue to bring about important changes in the size, structure and spatial distribution of families, households and communities around the world, creating both opportunities and challenges for the design of policies that aim to promote the well-being of current and future generations.

The demographic trends presented in this report are based for the most part on the results set out in *World Population Prospects: The 2012 Revision*, the twenty-third round of the official United Nations population estimates and projections prepared biennially by the Population Division of the Department of Economic and Social Affairs of the Secretariat. The 2012 revision builds on the previous revision by incorporating the results of new population census data from 94 countries and findings from many specialised demographic surveys that have been carried out around the world over the past several years. These data provide new information on population size and inform estimates of the three components of population change: fertility, mortality and migration.

Additional data for this report come from a number of other unique databases developed and maintained by the Population Division. Data on urban, rural and city populations are based on *World Urbanization Prospects: The 2011 Revision*, while data on contraceptive prevalence and unmet need for family planning are based on survey data from 194 countries or areas and on annual model-based estimates and short-term projections of family planning indicators, all

contained in *World Contraceptive Use 2012*. Estimates of the number of international migrants are based on *Trends in International Migrant Stock: The 2013 Revision*, which presents estimates of the number of migrants by origin, age and sex for each country and major area of the world.

Population size and growth

In 1994, when the international community met in Cairo at the International Conference on Population and Development, an estimated 5.7 billion people were living on the planet. At that time, nearly 84 million people were being added to the world's population annually. According to United Nations projections available at the time, the world's population was expected to grow by 87 million annually for the following 25 years. Whereas it had taken 123 years for the world's population to grow from one billion to two billion, it was projected at the time of the Cairo Conference that only 11 years would be required for the increase from five billion to six billion.

In 2014, the 20th anniversary of the Conference, the world's population has already surpassed 7 billion – a number reached in 2011 – even though it took a little longer than predicted in 1994, as population growth over the past 20 years has been slightly slower than expected. Between 2010 and 2014, the world's population grew at a rate of 1.2 per cent per annum, significantly below the 1.5 per cent per annum around the time of the Cairo Conference. At the beginning of 2014, the world's population was estimated at 7.2 billion, with approximately 82 million being added every year and roughly a quarter of this growth occurring in the least developed countries. On its current trajectory, the world's population is expected to reach 8.1 billion in 2025 and 9.6 billion in 2050.

While the absolute size of the world's population has grown substantially since the Cairo Conference, the annual increase in that population has been declining since the late 1960s. By 2050,

it is expected that the world's population will be growing by 49 million people per year, more than half of whom will live in the least developed countries. Currently, of the 82 million people added to the world's population every year, 54 per cent are in Asia and 33 per cent in Africa. By 2050, however, more than 80 per cent of the global increase will take place in Africa, with only 12 per cent in Asia.

Although most major areas experienced similar levels of population growth between 1994 and 2014, Africa and Europe stood out, with growth rates significantly higher in Africa and lower in Europe compared with other regions. Between 2014 and 2050, all major areas are expected to experience further reductions in their population growth rates, resulting in increasingly dramatic contrasts in population dynamics among them. For example, by 2050, Africa will be growing more than six times as fast as Latin America and the Caribbean and more than 15 times as fast as Asia. Partly because of international migration, the growth rates of both North America and Oceania will exceed those of Asia and Latin America and the Caribbean over the coming decades. Europe is projected to experience population decline after 2020. Overall, the global population growth rate is projected to fall to 0.5 per cent per annum by 2050.

Small variations in the trajectory of future fertility will have major consequences for the future size and structure of the world's population. In the high-fertility variant of the projections, an extra half child per woman, on average, implies that there would be 1.3 billion more people in the world in 2050 than under the medium-fertility variant. On the other hand, if women have, on average, a half child less, as implied by the low-fertility variant, there would be 1.2 billion fewer people in the world in 2050.

Most of the population growth projected to occur between 2014 and 2050 will be concentrated

in a small number of countries. During the period 2014–2050, nine countries are expected to account for more than half of the world's projected increase: the Democratic Republic of the Congo, Ethiopia, India, Indonesia, Nigeria, Pakistan, the United Republic of Tanzania, the United States of America and Uganda. Several of these countries are among the most populous today. Given its anticipated growth, India is projected to overtake China and become the world's most populous country by 2028. High population growth rates prevail in many of the countries that are on the United Nations list of 49 least developed countries. Between 2014 and 2050, the total population of these countries is projected to double, according to the medium-fertility variant, putting additional pressure on resources and the environment and straining government capacities to provide high-quality services.

At the other end of the spectrum, the populations of more than 40 countries and major areas are expected to decrease between 2014 and 2050. The largest absolute declines are expected for China, Germany, Japan, Poland, Romania, the Russian Federation, Serbia, Thailand and Ukraine. Many other countries, particularly in Eastern Europe, but also in East, South-East and Western Asia, other parts of Europe and Latin America and the Caribbean, are also expected to experience population decline before 2050. Population decline and the acceleration of population ageing are therefore important concerns in a growing number of countries and major areas.

2014

⇨ From *The World Population Situation in 2014: A Concise Report*, by the Department of Economic and Social Affairs Population Division, © 2014 United Nations. Reprinted with the permission of the United Nations.

Population ageing and sustainable development

Global ageing to accelerate in the coming decades

The percentage of the global population aged 60 years or over increased from 8.5 per cent in 1980 to 12.3 per cent in 2015 and is projected to rise further to 21.5 per cent in 2050.[1]

Out of 233 countries or areas, 191 (82 per cent) experienced increases in the proportion of older persons between 1980 and 2015. 231 countries or areas (99 per cent) are expected to see an increase in the proportion aged 60 or over between 2015 and 2050.

Population ageing is a phenomenon that results from declines in fertility as well as increases in longevity, two trends that are usually associated with social and economic development.

Europe was the first region to enter the demographic transition, having begun the shift to lower fertility and increasing longevity in the late 19th and early 20th centuries. As a result, today's European population is the most aged in the world, with 24 per cent of the population aged 60 or over. Europe is projected to remain the most aged region in the coming decades, with 34 per cent of the population projected to be aged 60 or over in 2050, followed by Northern America (27 per cent), Latin America and the Caribbean (25 per cent), Asia (24 per cent) and Oceania (23 per cent).

Compared to other regions, many parts of Africa entered the demographic transition relatively recently, and thus the ageing process has only just begun: older persons accounted for just over five per cent of the population of Africa in 2015, but that proportion is projected to nearly double by 2050.

Most of the projected growth of the older population will take place in the global South

1 Data are from World Population Prospects: The 2012 Revision, CD-ROM Edition-Extended Dataset (United Nations Publications, Sales No. 13.XIII.10)

Asia was home to more than half of the world's 901 million older persons in 2015, with 508 million people aged 60 or over. Another 177 million older persons resided in Europe (20 per cent), 75 million in Northern America (eight per cent), 71 million in Latin America and the Caribbean (eight per cent), 64 million in Africa (seven per cent), and six million in Oceania (one per cent).

By 2050 the number of older persons worldwide is projected to more than double to two billion. While that increase reflects growing numbers of older persons in all regions, Africa, Latin America and the Caribbean, and Asia are projected to see especially rapid growth of their older populations. The population of older persons in Africa is projected to more than triple by 2050, reaching 220 million. The number of older persons in Latin America and the Caribbean will nearly triple to 200 million in 2050 and the population aged 60 or over in Asia will more than double, reaching 1.3 billion by the mid-century. Between 2015 and 2050, the older populations of Europe and Northern America will grow by 38 per cent and 27 per cent, respectively, reaching 242 million and 123 million persons aged 60 or over.

The older population is itself ageing. Among those aged 60 or over worldwide, 14 per cent were aged 80 or over in 2015. By 2050,

the projected 434 million people aged 80 or over will account for 21 per cent of the global population over age 60.

The older population is and will remain predominantly female. Globally, women outlived men by 4.4 years on average between 2010 and 2015 (life expectancy at birth was 72.7 years for females compared to 68.3 years for males). As a result, women made up 54 per cent of those aged 60 or over and 61 per cent of those aged 80 or over.

As people age, they rely on various sources of financial support: labour income, assets, their families and public programmes

In developing countries, with limited public transfer systems, assets and labour income are the major sources of financial support for old age.[2] During their early old age (60–69 years), net asset reallocations together with labour income finance almost all of older persons' consumption. At more advanced ages (70 and over), these two sources continue to finance about 70 per cent of the consumption of older persons in developing

2 Data are obtained from National Transfer Accounts at www.ntaccounts.org. The developed countries in this sample include Austria, Germany, Hungary, Japan, Slovenia, Sweden and the United States of America. The sample of developing countries includes Brazil, China, Costa Rica, India, Indonesia, Mexico, the Republic of Korea, the Philippines and Thailand.

countries, while transfers (both public and private) become more important. In contrast, in the developed countries public transfers are a major source of old-age support, financing 39 per cent of the consumption among 60–69-year-olds and 67 per cent among those aged 70 years or over.

Older persons contribute financially to their families. Older persons are often net providers of financial transfers to their children and grandchildren in both developed and developing countries.

In developing countries, older persons aged 60 to 69 years give net financial transfers to younger generations in an amount equivalent to 28 per cent of older persons' consumption. They become net receivers of familial transfers only at more advanced ages (70 years or over), in an amount that accounts for 12 per cent of their consumption.

In the more developed countries, familial transfers comprise a smaller share of older persons' consumption even at more advanced ages: those aged 70 or over finance around seven per cent of their consumption, on average, through familial transfers.

Older persons increasingly are living independently. 40 per cent of the world's older population lives independently, that is, either alone or with a spouse only.[3] While the percentage living independently is similar by sex, higher female life expectancy means that older women are more likely to live alone (19 per cent) than older men (11 per cent).

Independent living is the dominant living arrangement of older persons in the more developed regions: almost three quarters of them live alone or with a spouse only. In contrast, less than 30 per cent of older persons in the less developed regions live independently. As populations continue to age, independent living is expected to become increasingly common among older persons in both the

Ageing population in the UK, 2014

- There were over half a million people aged 90 and over living in the United Kingdom (UK) in 2014.

- For every 100 men aged 90 and over in 2014 there were 249 women.

- The number of centenarians (people aged 100 and over) living in the UK has risen by 72% over the last decade to 14,450 in 2014.

- 780 of the 14,450 centenarians living in the UK in 2014 were estimated to be aged 105 or more, double the number in 2004.

- England and Wales had more centenarians per 100,000 population in 2014 than Scotland or Northern Ireland.

Source: Estimates of the Very Old (including Centenarians), England and Wales, and United Kingdom, 2002 to 2014, *Office for National Statistics*

more developed and less developed regions.

Healthcare systems must adapt to meet the changing needs of an ageing population

As populations age, non-communicable diseases (NCDs) account for a growing share of the overall disease burden, thereby confronting healthcare systems with new prevention and treatment challenges. The NCDs most associated with old age include cardiovascular diseases, cancers, diabetes and respiratory diseases, as well as other prominent causes of disability, such as arthritis, hearing and vision loss, depression, dementia and Alzheimer's disease.

While many countries have achieved reductions in the prevalence and severity of disability even as people survive to more advanced ages,[4] growth in the overall number of older persons has produced increases in the burden of NCD-related disability. The years of life lost due to disability (YLD) is a metric that summarises both the prevalence and severity of disability experienced in a population. The countries that saw the largest increases in the population aged 60 or over between 2000 and 2012 – most of which are

located in Africa, Asia and Latin America and the Caribbean – also tended to experience larger proportional increases in the years of life lost due to NCD-related disability.

As the population of older persons continues to grow into the future, so too will the demand for interventions that prevent and treat morbidities associated with old age. Preventing disease and postponing morbidity to later ages can both improve older persons' quality of life and mitigate future increases in healthcare costs implied by population ageing. Nevertheless, apart from population ageing, income growth and technological advances in medicine are anticipated to continue to exert substantial upward pressure on health expenditures in many countries.[5]

5 October 2015

⇨ The above information is reprinted with kind permission from the UN. Please visit www.un.org for further information.

© *UN 2015*

3 United Nations (2013). World Population Ageing 2013, available from www.unpopulation.org.

4 Christensen, K., G. Doblhammer, R. Rau and J.W. Vaupel (2009). Ageing populations: the challenges ahead, The Lancet, vol. 374, No. 9696, pp. 1196-1208.

5 WHO (2011). Global health and ageing: brief report.

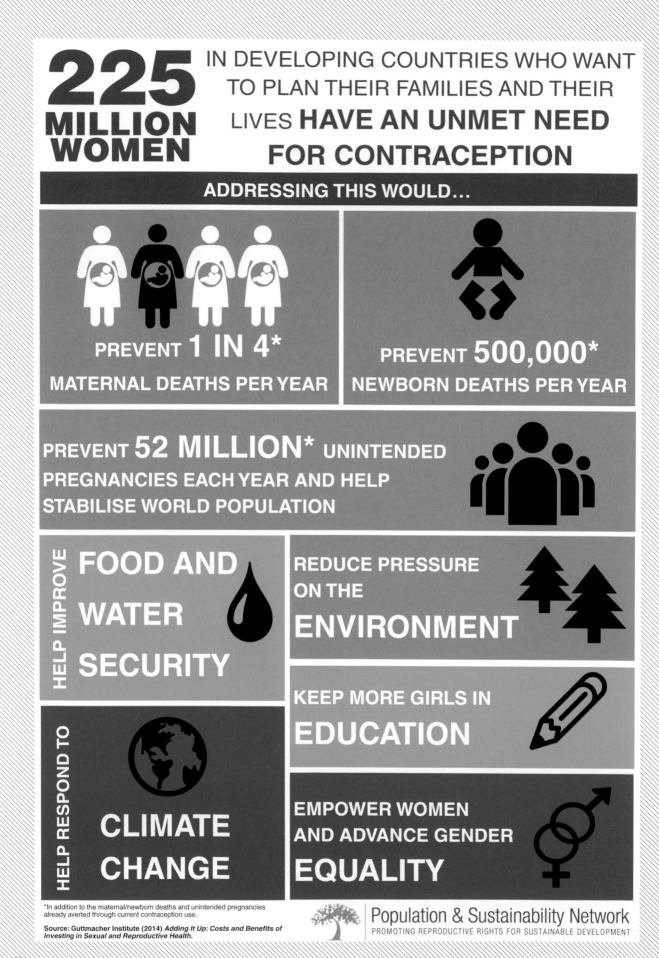

225 MILLION WOMEN

IN DEVELOPING COUNTRIES WHO WANT TO PLAN THEIR FAMILIES AND THEIR LIVES HAVE AN UNMET NEED FOR CONTRACEPTION

ADDRESSING THIS WOULD...

PREVENT **1 IN 4***
MATERNAL DEATHS PER YEAR

PREVENT **500,000***
NEWBORN DEATHS PER YEAR

PREVENT **52 MILLION*** UNINTENDED PREGNANCIES EACH YEAR AND HELP STABILISE WORLD POPULATION

HELP IMPROVE **FOOD AND WATER SECURITY**

REDUCE PRESSURE ON THE **ENVIRONMENT**

KEEP MORE GIRLS IN **EDUCATION**

HELP RESPOND TO **CLIMATE CHANGE**

EMPOWER WOMEN AND ADVANCE GENDER **EQUALITY**

*In addition to the maternal/newborn deaths and unintended pregnancies already averted through current contraception use.

Source: Guttmacher Institute (2014) *Adding It Up: Costs and Benefits of Investing in Sexual and Reproductive Health.*

Population & Sustainability Network
PROMOTING REPRODUCTIVE RIGHTS FOR SUSTAINABLE DEVELOPMENT

⇨ The above infographic is reprinted with kind permission from the Population & Sustainability Network. Please visit www.populationandsustainability.org for further information.

The world at 2035 – who are the extra two billion?

It is widely reported that the global population will continue to increase over the next two–three decades until it stabilises at close to nine billion (from today's seven billion). However, what is less clear is who these "extra" two billion will be...

Where will they live?

Opposite we have provided a summary table of estimated population growth by region, however within these numbers there are a number of interesting trends:

1. Fast-growing African and Asian Cities – the most significant population growth will occur in East and West Africa and Southern Asia, notably within cities. For instance: Nigeria's population is estimated to grow by 109 million (from 179–288 million); Tanzania's from 52 to 94 million; the population of Pakistan will increase by 57 million (the equivalent to an additional United Kingdom).

2. Europe and North America – A tale of two cities (forgotten fities and global cities): at first glance there appears to be little population change in Europe and North America, but this masks an important dynamic. On one hand, it is expected that high-profile global cities such as London and New York will continue to grow in population and continue to dominate the economies in which they are located. In parallel, fuelled by out-sourcing of labour and the pull of global mega-cities (as above), industrial and planned cities are likely to contract in size, as witnessed by Detroit in the early 2000s. Czech Republic, Estonia, Latvia, Poland and Slovakia are all predicted negative urbanisation

3. Medium-size cities – leading to sprawling: The fastest growing urban agglomerations between 2005 and 2015 were cities with less than one million inhabitants. This trend is predicted to continue, such that cities will begin to merge creating new sprawling urban zones – for instance along the coasts of Western Africa and Southern Asia.

	Population 2015	Population 2035	Change
World	7.28 billion	8.61 billion	+ 1.33 billion
Africa	1.15 billion	1.72 billion	+0.57 billion
Eastern Africa	0.37 billion	0.59 billion	+0.22 billion
Middle Africa	0.14 billion	0.22 billion	+0.08 billion
Northern Africa	0.23 billion	0.29 billion	+0.06 billion
Southern Africa	0.06 billion	0.07 billion	+0.01 billion
Western Africa	0.35 billion	0.55 billion	+0.20 billion
Asia	4.37 billion	4.99 billion	+0.62 billion
Eastern Asia	1.60 billion	1.61 billion	+0.01 billion
Centra Asia	0.06 billion	0.08 billion	+0.02 billion
Southern Asia	1.83 billion	2.23 billion	+0.40 billion
South-Eastern Asia	0.63 billion	0.73 billion	+0.10 billion
Western Asia	0.25 billion	0.34 billion	+0.10 billion
Latin & South America	0.62 billion	0.72 billion	+0.10 billion
Caribbean	0.04 billion	0.05 billion	+0.01 billion
Central America	0.17 billion	0.20 billion	+0.03 billion
South America	0.41 billion	0.47 billion	+0.06 billion
North America	0.36 billion	0.41 billion	+0.05 billion
Europe	0.74 billion	0.72 billion	-0.02 billion
Eastern Europe	0.29 billion	0.27 billion	-0.02 billion
Northern Europe	0.10 billion	0.11 billion	+0.01 billion
Southern Europe	0.16 billion	0.16 billion	0.00 billion
Western Europe	0.19 billion	0.19 billion	0.00 billion
Oceania	0.04 billion	0.05 billion	+0.01 billion

So what could this mean?

With more people living in cities on the coast, the impact of climate change and predicted sea-level rise could be disastrous, e.g. over 23% of the world's population lives within coastal-flood zones.

New public health crises – with more people living in closer proximity and new demands placed on sanitation, the potential for global health crises will continue to rise, e.g. as witnessed by the recent Ebola outbreak in Western Africa.

With ever greater populations in urban zones, ever more food and resources will need to be produced and transported into cities – requiring increased efficiency and new innovative solutions, e.g. vertical farming.

New consumer markets will open up, with an 'affluent' lower- to middle-class emerging across Africa and Southern Asia, e.g. by 2030 Africa's top 18 cities will have a combined spending power of $1.3 trillion.

Sources

⇨ Greenpeace 2012

⇨ United Nations Department of Economic and Social Affairs (DESA)

⇨ United Nations Statistics Division *6 April 2015*

⇨ The above information is reprinted with kind permission from Article 13. Please visit www.article13.com for further information.

© Article 13 2015

Migration

Population growth and migration

The recent surge in refugees trying to reach Europe has brought renewed attention to the conflicts and power struggles occurring in the Middle East and North Africa. Very often a major contributor to the instability – one that commonly is overlooked – is population growth.

The situation in Syria is a perfect example. The country experienced a drought in 2009. This coupled with rapid population growth and insufficient resources to satisfy the needs of all contributed to the unstable situation that led to popular uprisings. Climate change also was a factor. Increased temperatures and harsher weather conditions exacerbated the negative impacts of the drought.

A related problem often created by population growth is 'youth bulge'. When large populations of young people are present in weak or autocratic states, unrest often ensues. As states fail to provide employment opportunities, access to resources and services such as education and healthcare, discontent and instability occur – particularly amongst younger people. This typically leads to young people seeking more secure means of providing for themselves and their families elsewhere.

Most countries categorised as 'weak and under stress' by the World Bank are nations that have experienced rapid increases in population.

"Overpopulation in states unable to provide for the needs of their citizens is very likely to create large waves of migration to wealthier countries," said Population Matters Chief Executive Simon Ross.

Conflict and migration

Conflict is one response to scarcity of resources. Although a lack of resources is rarely stated as the justification for war, such lack is often an underlying factor. Intercountry and civil war are the most extreme cases, but many lesser forms of conflict – food riots, for example – also can arise when resources are in short supply.

Competition for resources resulting from population growth can engender conflict and disruption arising from conflict can in turn reduce access to family planning services. Failed and fragile states do typically have a high birth rate.

Migration is another response. Global migration is at record levels and likely to increase still further as population growth, increased exploitation and climate change increase pressure on resources – particularly fisheries. Increasing unemployment in poorer countries will lead growing numbers to seek a better life abroad.

Migration can bring benefits to both individuals and countries. The individual can gain access to new opportunities and the country of origin receives monies sent back to relatives. Some countries rely on such remittances for a large proportion of their income. Likewise, the country of destination obtains skills and labour.

Large-scale and persistent net immigration can result in an imbalance between demand for consumption and sustainable resources. These flows of people represent a humanitarian crisis and put pressure on the sustainability of destination countries. Migrants from poor to rich countries increase their own consumption levels to match the unsustainable levels of their adopted country. Sustained net migration therefore exacerbates global unsustainability.

Countries throughout the world are responding to higher population levels and increasing migration by limiting immigration. No matter what level is set, policies should be applied in a humane and nondiscriminatory manner and the right to asylum of those in fear should be maintained.

We believe the only just and long-term solution to migration pressure is to address its underlying causes in the countries of origin, such as poverty, lack or overexploitation of resources, climate change and conflict. Developed countries have a clear moral responsibility to help with this because they contribute to migratory pressure by being both major consumers of resources from developing countries and the principal source of the causes of climate change.

For countries that have an ecological footprint larger than their carrying capacity, we propose limiting immigration to the extent necessary to allow population numbers to decrease gradually to a sustainable level.

⇨ The above information is reprinted with kind permission from Population Matters. Please visit www.populationmatters.org for further information.

© Population Matters 2015

The Mediterranean's deadliest migration sea routes

As 400 migrants – including children – are feared to have died after a boat capsized off Libya, Channel 4 News looks at the desperate journeys migrants are taking to reach Europe.

The boat, carrying about 550 migrants in total, flipped 24 hours after leaving the Libyan coast, according to some of the 150 survivors who were rescued. The survivors were mostly Sub-Saharan Africans.

Officials say there has been a marked rise in the number of people trying to sail from the north African coast to Europe, with 8,500 rescued from the sea since Friday say the UN Refugee Agency (UNHCR).

With summer approaching, over 500,000 people are waiting to set out from Libya, according to EU border agency Frontex. However, migrants are also using other sea routes to get to their destinations.

Central Mediterranean route

This is the name of the migratory flow coming from northern Africa towards Italy and Malta through the Mediterranean Sea. For years, this route has been an important entry point for irregular migrants to the EU, and in 2008, nearly 40,000 of them were detected.

These were mainly nationals from Tunisia, Nigeria, Somalia and Eritrea. However, this movement stopped almost completely in 2009 after the Italian Government signed a bilateral agreement with Libya.

This changed in 2011, when the eruption of civil unrest in Tunisia and Libya created a massive spike in the number of migrants to more than 64,000 along this route.

With the collapse of the Gaddafi regime in August 2011, the migratory pressure dropped almost entirely, and detections in 2012 remained very low. But the following year saw a second peak in the departures from Libya.

The dramatic conditions of the overcrowded boats used by the migrants were particularly visible in October 2013, when 366 migrants lost their lives near Lampedusa when their boat suddenly capsized.

In 2014, detections in the Central Mediterranean area reached a staggering level. More than 170,000 migrants arrived in Italy alone. Many migrants have come from Libya, where the lack of rule of law and basic law enforcement allow smuggling networks to thrive.

Syrians and Eritreans were the top two nationalities to have travelled to Italy by sea, but numerous Africans coming from Sub-Saharan regions also use this route.

The increasing number of migrants departing from northern Africa also led to an increase in the number of people who perished at sea. According to UNHCR, in 2014 some 3,500 migrants lost their lives while crossing the Mediterranean.

Apulia and Calabria route

This route refers to irregular migration coming from Turkey and Egypt and also includes the migratory movements between Greece and Italy. The types of the vessels detected in the Ionian Sea are different from the ones used on other maritime borders – the smugglers tend to use yachts rather than fishing boats.

The smugglers on board the sailing boats are the only people visible while navigating and are sometimes accompanied by women in order to avoid attracting the attention of the patrolling authorities. All migrants tend to be hidden below deck in overcrowded conditions with insufficient ventilation.

Smuggling networks from Egypt, on the other hand, typically make use of larger 'mother ships.' Rather than setting off from Egypt in fishing boats, the new method sees bigger vessels carrying larger numbers of migrants, towing fishing boats behind them.

Once close enough to shore, the migrants are transferred to the fishing boats for the remainder of the journey while the mother ship returns to port. The main nationalities using this route include Syrians, but also Afghans, Pakistanis and Bangladeshis.

In 2014, the smugglers started using much larger boats from Turkey – decommissioned cargo vessels departing mainly from the Turkish port of Mersin towards Italy. The profits the smugglers make using this method are staggering considering that on average the Syrians are charged about £5,000 each for the service.

With freighters frequently filled with as many as 600 people, the revenue of the smugglers runs into the millions. Travelling this way not only circumvents the considerable danger of capsizing in a small boat in rough seas: it also avoids having to go to Libya.

The new route from Turkey is not without dangers however. The engines of the old ships are often highly unreliable. The danger of shipwreck is greatly increased by the smugglers' habit of switching off the freighter's AIS (the Automatic Identification System) to make the boat electronically invisible to the authorities but also to other boats and vessels navigating on the Mediterranean Sea.

On numerous occasions, the crew would set the vessels on autopilot and either abandon the boat or hide among other passengers to avoid arrest.

15 April 2015

⇨ The above information is reprinted with kind permission from Channel 4 News. Please visit www.channel4.com for further information.

© *Channel 4 2015*

The future of cities: what is the global agenda?

An extract from the report commissioned as part of the UK Government's Foresight Future of Cities Project.

By Emily Moir, Tim Moonen and Greg Clark

What will the urbanised world of the future look like?

By 2050, it is expected that nearly 70% of the world's population will live in urban areas. Recent reports by the UN anticipate some of the key differences between today's urban world and that of 2050:

There will be more cities...

The UN recorded that there were 1,551 cities worldwide in 2010. By 2030, that number is expected to have surpassed 2,000, with continuing growth to 2050. Cities of all sizes are expected to continue to grow in number. For example, whilst there are 43 'large cities' with populations between five and ten million in 2014, there are expected to be 63 by 2030.

...including more mega-cities.

The UN estimates that there will be more than 40 mega-cities worldwide by 2030, each with a population of at least ten million, compared to 28 today. It is thought that Delhi, Shanghai and Tokyo will each have more than 30 million people by 2030, and will be the world's largest urban agglomerations.

More people will live in bigger cities

Overall, 2.5 billion people will be added to the world's urban population by 2050. Today, almost half of the world's urban population live in cities with populations of less than 500,000. More people will continue to live in these smaller cities than in any other city type, but their share of urban dwellers is expected to shrink over time.

Urbanisation will continue to be an uneven process

Almost all (nearly 90%) of the increase in urban population by 2050 is expected to be concentrated in Asia and Africa. By 2050, most of the world's urban population will be concentrated in Asia (52%) and Africa (21%). In more advanced nations, urban population growth is almost stagnant (0.67% on an annual average basis since 2010), and in some cases is even decreasing: Japan is expected to lose 12 million urban dwellers by 2050 and the Russian Federation's urban population is expected to decline by seven million people. By comparison, the aggregate annual population increase in six major developing country cities – New Delhi and Mumbai, Dhaka, Lagos, Kinshasa and Karachi – is greater than Europe's entire population.

Even within the developing world, some regions will experience more rapid and widespread urbanisation than others

Africa will be the world's most rapidly urbanising continent between 2014 and 2050. It is projected to experience a 16% rise in its urban population – bringing the percentage of people living in its cities to 56%. Paradoxically, this degree of urbanisation will still result in it being one of the least urbanised regions of the world. The fastest growing cities are, and will continue to be medium sized cities and cities with fewer than one million inhabitants, located in Asia and Africa. Just three countries – India, China and Nigeria – are expected to account for 37% of the world's urban growth between 2014 and 2050.

As such, global urbanisation presents a very wide range of different contexts for considering the future of cities.

September 2014

⇨ The above information is reprinted with kind permission from the Government Office for Science. Please visit www.gov. uk for further information.

Can the Earth feed 11 billion people? Four reasons to fear a Malthusian future

An article from The Conversation.

THE CONVERSATION

By James Dyke, Lecturer in Complex Systems Simulation, University of Southampton

Humanity is on course for a population greater than 11 billion by the end of this century, according to the latest analysis from the UN's population division.

In a simple sense, population is the root cause of all sustainability issues. Clearly if there were no humans there would be no human impacts. Assuming you don't wish to see the complete end of the human race – a desire that is shared by some deep green thinkers and Bond super-villians – then the issue is whether there is an optimal number of humans on the planet.

Discussions on population growth often start with the work of Rev. Thomas Robert Malthus whose *An Essay on the Principle of Population* published at the end of the 18th century is one of the seminal works of demography. Populations change in response to three driving factors: fertility – how many people are born; mortality – how many people die; and migration – how many people leave or enter the population.

Malthus observed that more births than deaths would lead to exponential growth which would always outpace any improvements in farming and increases in yields. Consequently, unchecked growth was doomed to end in famine and population collapse. Malthus was right about exponential growth, but he was famously wrong about his dire predictions for the consequences of such growth.

At a global level we can ignore migration (no interplanetary migration happening just yet) and so the tremendous rise in the total numbers of humans is a result of an imbalance between fertility and mortality rates.

Over longer timescales, the recent increases look practically vertiginous. We seem to be on a trajectory that would surely exceed whatever the carrying capacity of the Earth is. However, 11 billion could be the high water mark as the UN forecasts population to slowly decrease after the end of this century.

This brings us to Malthus' first error: he wasn't able to appreciate that the process of industrialisation and development that decreased mortality rates would, in time, decrease fertility rates too. Higher living standards associated with better education, in particular female education and empowerment, seem to lead to smaller family sizes – a demographic transition that has played out with some variations across most of the countries around the world.

This may explain how populations can overcome unsustainable growth, but it still seems remarkable that the Earth can provide for a 700% increase in the numbers of humans over the span of less than a few centuries. This was Malthus's second error. He simply couldn't conceive of the tremendous increases in yields that industrialisation produced.

How we fed seven billion

The 'green revolution' that produced a four-fold increase in global food productivity since the middle of the 20th century relied on irrigation, pesticides and fertilisers.

You may describe yourself as an omnivore, vegetarian, or vegan – but in a sense we all eat fossilised carbon. This is because most fertiliser is produced through the Haber process which creates ammonia (a fertiliser) by reacting atmospheric nitrogen with hydrogen under

high temperatures and pressures. All that heat requires serious amounts of energy, and the hydrogen is derived from natural gas, which currently means the Haber process uses lots of fossil fuels. If we include production, processing, packaging, transportation, marketing and consumption, then the food system consumes more than 30% of total energy use while contributing 20% to global greenhouse gas emissions.

Feeding the next four billion

If industrialised agriculture can now feed seven billion, then why can't we figure out how to feed 11 billion by the end of this century? There may be many issues that need to be addressed, the argument runs, but famine isn't one of them. However, there are a number of potentially unpleasant problems with this prognosis.

First, some research suggests global food production is stagnating. The green revolution hasn't run out of steam just yet but innovations such as GM crops, more efficient irrigation and subterranean farming aren't going to have a big enough impact. The low-hanging fruits of yield improvements have already been gobbled up.

Second, the current high yields assume plentiful and cheap supplies of phosphorus, nitrogen and fossil fuels – mainly oil and gas. Mineral phosphorus isn't going to run out anytime soon, nor will oil, but both are becoming increasingly harder to obtain. All things being equal this will make them more expensive. The chaos in the world food systems in 2007–8 gives some indication of the impact of higher food prices.

Third, soil is running out. Or rather it is running away. Intensive agriculture, which plants crops on fields without respite, leads to soil erosion. This can be offset by using more fertiliser, but there comes a point where the soil is so eroded that farming there becomes very limited, and it will take many years for such soils to recover.

Fourth, it is not even certain we will be able to maintain yields in a world that is facing potentially significant environmental change. We are on course towards 2°C of warming by the end of this century. Just when we have the greatest numbers of people to feed, floods, storms, droughts and other extreme weather will cause significant disruption to food production. In order to avoid dangerous climate change, we must keep the majority of the Earth's fossil fuel deposits in the ground – the same fossil fuels that our food production system has become effectively addicted to.

If humanity is to have a long-term future, we must address all these challenges at the same time as reducing our impacts on the planetary processes that ultimately provide not just the food we eat, but water we drink and air we breathe. This is a challenge far greater than those that so exercised Malthus 200 years ago.

12 August 2015

⇨ The above information is reprinted with kind permission from *The Conversation*. Please visit www.theconversation.com for further information.

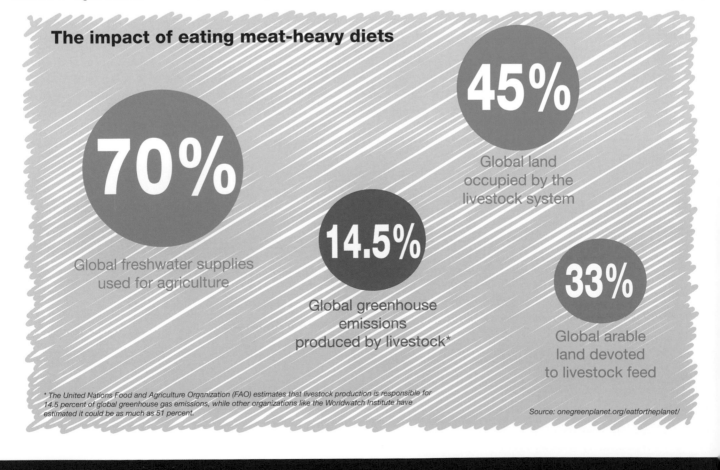

The impact of eating meat-heavy diets

70%
Global freshwater supplies used for agriculture

45%
Global land occupied by the livestock system

14.5%
Global greenhouse emissions produced by livestock*

33%
Global arable land devoted to livestock feed

* The United Nations Food and Agriculture Organization (FAO) estimates that livestock production is responsible for 14.5 percent of global greenhouse gas emissions, while other organizations like the Worldwatch Institute have estimated it could be as much as 51 percent.

Source: onegreenplanet.org/eatfortheplanet/

There's a population crisis all right. But probably not the one you think

While all eyes are on human numbers, it's the rise in farm animals that is laying the planet waste.

By George Monbiot

This article is about the population crisis. About the breeding that's laying waste the world's living systems. But it's probably not the population crisis you're thinking of. This is about another one, that we seem to find almost impossible to discuss.

You'll hear a lot about population in the next three weeks, as the Paris climate summit approaches. Across the airwaves and on the comment threads it will invariably be described as "the elephant in the room". When people are not using their own words, it means that they are not thinking their own thoughts. 10,000 voices each ask why no one is talking about it. The growth in human numbers, they say, is our foremost environmental threat.

At their best, population campaigners seek to extend women's reproductive choices. Some 225 million women have an unmet need for contraception. If this need were answered, the impact on population growth would be significant, though not decisive: the annual growth rate of 83 million would be reduced to 62 million. But contraception is rarely limited only by the physical availability of contraceptives. In most cases it's about power: women are denied control of their wombs. The social transformations that they need are wider and deeper than donations from the other side of the world are likely to achieve.

At their worst, population campaigners seek to shift the blame from their own environmental impacts. Perhaps it's no coincidence that so many post-reproductive white men are obsessed with human population growth, as it's about the only environmental problem of which they can wash their hands. Nor, I believe, is it a coincidence that of all such topics this is the least tractable. When there is almost nothing to be done, there is no requirement to act.

Such is the momentum behind population growth, an analysis in the *Proceedings of the National Academy of Sciences* discovered, that were every government to adopt the one-child policy China has just abandoned, there would still be as many people on Earth at the end of this century as there are today. If two billion people were wiped out by a catastrophe mid-century, the planet would still hold a billion more by 2100 than it does now.

If we want to reduce our impacts this century, the paper concludes, it is consumption we must address. Population growth is outpaced by the growth in our consumption of almost all resources. There is enough to meet everyone's need, even in a world of ten billion people. There is not enough to meet everyone's greed, even in a world of two billion people.

So let's turn to a population crisis over which we do have some influence. I'm talking about the growth in livestock numbers. Human numbers are rising at roughly 1.2% a year, while livestock numbers are rising at around 2.4% a year. By 2050 the world's living systems will have to support about 120 million tonnes of extra humans, and 400 million tonnes of extra farm animals.

Raising these animals already uses three-quarters of the world's agricultural land. A third of our cereal crops are used to feed livestock: this may rise to roughly half by 2050. More people will starve as a result, because the poor rely mainly on grain for their subsistence, and diverting it to livestock raises the price. And now the grain that farm animals consume is being supplemented by oil crops, particularly soya, for which the forests and savannahs of South America are being cleared at shocking rates.

This might seem counter-intuitive, but were we to eat soya rather than meat, the clearance of natural vegetation required to supply us with the same amount of protein would decline by 94%. Producing protein from chickens requires three times as much land as protein from soybeans. Pork needs nine times, beef 32 times.

A recent paper in the journal *Science of the Total Environment* suggests that our consumption of meat is likely to be "the leading cause of modern species extinctions". Not only is livestock farming the major reason for habitat destruction and the killing of predators, but its waste products are overwhelming the world's capacity to absorb them. Factory farms in the US generate 13 times as much sewage as the human population does. The dairy farms in Tulare County, California, produce five times as much as New York City.

Freshwater life is being wiped out across the world by farm manure. In England, the system designed to protect us from the tide of slurry has comprehensively broken down. Dead zones now extend from many coasts, as farm sewage erases ocean life across thousands of square kilometres.

Livestock farming creates around 14% of the world's greenhouse gas emissions: slightly more than the output of the world's cars, lorries, buses, trains, ships and planes. If you eat soya, your emissions per unit of protein are 20 times lower than eating pork or chicken, and 150 times lower than eating beef.

So why is hardly anyone talking about the cow, pig, sheep and chicken in the room? Why are there no government campaigns to reduce the consumption of animal products, just as they sometimes discourage our excessive use of electricity?

A survey by the Royal Institute of International Affairs found that people are not unwilling to change diets once they become aware of the problem, but that many have no idea that livestock farming damages the living world.

It's not as if eating less meat and dairy will harm us. If we did as our doctors advise, our environmental impacts would decline in step with heart disease, strokes, diabetes and cancer. British people eat, on average, slightly more than their body weight in meat every year, while Americans consume another 50%: wildly more, in both cases, than is good for us or the rest of life on Earth.

But while plenty in the rich world are happy to discuss the dangers of brown people reproducing, the other population crisis scarcely crosses the threshold of perception. Livestock numbers present a direct moral challenge, as in this case we have agency. Hence the pregnant silence.

19 November 2015

⇨ The above information is reprinted with kind permission from *The Guardian*. Please visit www.theguardian.com for further information.

The hypocrisy at the heart of today's food security debate

By Jonathon Porritt

On David Attenborough's 89th birthday this May, he somehow found himself in conversation with Barack Obama. And a rather strange conversation it was too, with the President of the United States somehow more in awe of David Attenborough than the other way round!

For an old population hand (and fellow Patron of Population Matters), what really impressed me was that David Attenborough managed to squeeze in two forthright references to population during the conversation. Barack Obama had little to say in reply, but at least the BBC kept those references in, without exercising a rather more familiar editorial line which sees any and every reference to population as either insignificant or politically suspicious.

After 40 years on the population front line, even I am getting a little bit worn down by the 'COCCOP Factor' when it comes to dealing with population in the media: the Collective Censorship Consensus on Population has been so effective at shutting population out of mainstream debate that I suspect most people (even compassionate, intelligent, plugged-in people) just don't understand how every single one of their hopes and aspirations for the future of humankind are rendered entirely null and void by the inability/refusal of humankind to address the challenge of restricting further population growth.

Take food security, for instance. The quality of today's debate about food security is laughable.

1. Only in the last couple of years have policy-makers and scientists begun to acknowledge that it makes little sense talking about doubling the amount of food we'll need in order to avert mass famine when roughly half the food grown today never ends up passing through a human being's digestive tract. The consequences of this from the point of view of soil erosion, water shortages, biodiversity, pollution and climate change are quite staggering. According to a recent article on the Triple Pundit website, if the phenomenon of food waste was treated like a separate country, it would be responsible for the emission of more greenhouse gases than all the countries in the world put together except China and the USA.

2. Only now are we beginning to understand that there's a world of difference between the goal of providing enough protein for nine billion people by 2050 and seeking to achieve that goal with meat as the primary source of that protein. Today's meat-intensive diets and long-term food security for humankind are (literally) mutually exclusive. Yet time after time, one ends up listening to experts on food security get through an entire lecture without once mentioning the fact that we cannot possibly sustain current levels of meat consumption.

3. Most of the prescriptions that world leaders advocate in terms of doubling the amount of food required to 'feed the world' are oblivious to the impact of those prescriptions on soil quality, water consumption, energy balances, emissions of greenhouse gases and biodiversity. In other words, in a rapidly-warming, water-constrained, eroding world, heading inexorably towards an extinction spasm of some kind, such prescriptions are wholly

duplicitous and almost wholly irrelevant.

Do you see how I haven't even mentioned population yet? But just imagine that we started to have a rather more intelligent debate about food security. That we started to prioritise policies that addressed the first of those three challenges – which is wholly doable, by the way, and is at long last creeping into mainstream policy portfolios. That we then started to talk seriously about the second challenge – still a bit 'out there' at the moment, but not as far beyond the pale of rational debate as it once was. And that we then started to invest in the kind of global research programmes to address the third of those challenges, which would help bring the concept of truly sustainable food security back within the bounds of physical reality.

Even then, EVEN THEN, you'd still have to ask whether that emerging, much, much smarter approach to policy would provide enough protein and enough good nutritious food for at least nine billion people by 2050.

So why are we so ill-served by the very experts on whom our future depends? The truth of it is that most agronomists (let alone economists and policy wonks) live in the Land of Nod when it comes to addressing food security on a genuinely sustainable basis, taking human numbers properly into account rather than treating them as an irrelevance.

But at least those experts have got a few empirical datasets to work with to provide a patina of would-be realism. Which is a lot more than can be said for most of the world's political and religious leaders.

And since the world is still agog with excitement at the recent papal encyclical (taking the strongest possible line on the need to address accelerating climate change from a moral perspective), let's dwell for a moment on the continuing failure of the Catholic Church to change its archaic and fundamentally inhumane position on family planning and on the rights of women anywhere in the world to have access to a choice of artificial contraception.

The Catholic Church is quite properly concerned about world hunger, and the worsening threats to food security. But it still fails to see any connection between those concerns and the sheer number of human beings on planet Earth.

In his encyclical, the Pope fell back on that tired old either/or story (overpopulation versus overconsumption): "To blame population growth (for climate change) instead of extreme consumerism on the part of some is one way of refusing to face the issues." As is blaming extreme consumerism instead of population growth! Carl Safina captured the absurdity of this position in an excellent blog for The Huffington Post back in June:

"Human stress on the world results from what people do and how many people do it. Rich people have a disproportionately negative effect per person, but there are many poor people whose smaller personal damage to forests, wild creatures, reefs and waters all adds up. Certainly the rampant wastefulness of so-called 'developed societies' must be tamed. Yet in many of those same developed societies, population growth has greatly slowed because of progress in gender equality and female empowerment, where the Catholic Church continues to lag far behind."

One of the things that has most astonished me over the last 40 years is the comparison that can be drawn between the position of the Catholic Church and the position of most environmental NGOs. The continuing refusal of the vast majority of those NGOs to address the challenge of population growth is no less absurd than that of the Pope – without the excuse of being bound by centuries of implacable, intelligence-bypassing dogma.

(The results of a fascinating exercise ranking some of the most prominent NGOs operating in the UK on their responses to this challenge are illuminating.)

And that's what makes David Attenborough such an important contributor to this debate. Almost without exception, he is held in the highest esteem by those NGOs, but they'd probably be rather less impressed by his trenchant views on population, the environment and economic development – if they ever took the trouble to listen to those views.

The simple truth is that trying to address issues like food security without even engaging in the debate about population is pure, unadulterated hypocrisy.

24 July 2015

⇨ The above information is reprinted with kind permission from the Sustainable Food Trust. Please visit www.sustainablefoodtrust.org for further information.

Population debate: why the Pope needs encouragement, not criticism

Chief Executive Patrick Holden responds to last week's article by Jonathon Porritt on overpopulation and his criticism of the Pope.

Dear Jonathon,

Thank you so much for responding to my invitation to share your views about the problem of overpopulation for the SFT website.

As someone who has played a part in contributing to overpopulation, with eight children to my name, I confess, at least in part, to have been a significant contributor to this problem! However, without wanting to let myself, the environmental NGOs or the Catholic Church off the hook, I think it is worth reflecting why it is that so many institutions and individuals end up sticking to outdated orthodoxies.

I'm no expert in the history of why and when it came to pass that the Catholic Church took the view that the sanctity of life commenced with conception, and that taking steps to prevent conception was wrong. However, trying for a moment to put myself in the Pope's shoes, I can easily imagine how difficult it must be for him to abandon one of the defining precepts of Catholicism. For him, this must surely not just be a moral but also a political dilemma – how can he take it upon himself to decide which elements of Catholicism should be superseded by changing events and which elements are sacred?

That's the moral part of the dilemma, but politically, if he decides to change his stance, presumably he also risks an enormous backlash from the establishment element of his church. In saying this I'm not trying to defend the Pope, as I completely agree with you that until and unless the world deals with our collective problem of an ever-growing population on a finite planet, any efforts we make to be more sustainable will be overwhelmed by the sheer scale of demand and exceed all so-called planetary boundaries.

However, I know from my own experience that having the courage to abandon a principle, an ideology, a truth which is held to be of central importance by a whole movement, is not so easy and I'm wondering whether 'hypocrisy' is quite the right word to use when one is trying to encourage individuals in leadership positions to embark on that lonely journey?

You may recall occasions in the past when you have attacked me for a rigid adherence to the belief that organic farming, which as you know I helped to develop and promote while I was at the Soil Association, is the only way forward for global food production. Organic farming was conceived as a way of making food production more sustainable, yet I have finally reached the conclusion that, although I remain absolutely committed to the principles of organic farming, unfortunately the motives behind the organic project, at least in the UK, have been misinterpreted and misunderstood. My advocacy played a part in polarising the food community into those that are and those that aren't organic and that has not been helpful in addressing the problems on the major part of farmed land.

I can now see that almost all farmers want to farm in a sustainable way, but many of them have become locked into their damaging production systems by financial constraints. As such, I'm now more keen to work with them to help find a way forward, than to criticise them because they can't see a way out. And with the Pope having taken such important steps on the environment, as you recognise, maybe trying to find a way to work with him and broaden the definition of the sanctity of life, rather than simply oppose him on this matter, would bear more fruit?

But what are the key ingredients necessary for this to happen? Arguably it needs courage and humility in equal measure, but also perhaps a reconciling gesture from those that are leading the call for change? I know there is a counter argument here, namely that we need people, in this case you, to call a spade a spade, as you have done so brilliantly on so many fronts over

the years. But sometimes that can exacerbate the barrier of pride; and that to me suggests we need rescuers as well as persecutors!

In response to the other issue you raise, namely whether and how we can feed the eventual peak population, I agree strongly with you on the points you make about waste. But even if we sorted this out, without making fundamental changes to agricultural practices, we will only push soils, the finite resource upon which almost all food production depends, towards collapse at an even faster rate than we are doing already.

As I know you are aware, from a report you wrote back in the 1980s, farmers have been mining soil fertility with continuous crop production fuelled by chemical fertilisers and pesticides across the globe. This has already created a situation where more than half of all soils are moderately or severely degraded. For every adult and child on the planet three and a half tonnes of soil is irrevocably lost each year. Inevitably, degraded and eroded soils will produce less not more food in future.

Some people might assume that farmers could just stop using these chemicals and still maintain continuous crop production, but that simply isn't the case; it needs a complete change of approach. Of most significance, is the loss of organic matter, and with it the release of yet more carbon and nitrogen from the soil to the atmosphere, which is both contributing to climate change and making soils far less resilient to the increasing extremes of weather already being experienced in many parts of the world. Soils with low organic matter levels rapidly suffer from drought during dry periods, and are also more vulnerable to erosion during both drought and heavy rain.

To address this and feed what will hopefully be a reduced peak population as a result of your advocacy, we have need to reverse this decline in soil organic matter. To do that we need to return all the world's arable soils to more diverse forms of farming, including crop rotations with a fertility building phase, which will normally include grazed grasses

and forage legumes, in other words cellulose plant material which can only be digested by ruminants.

This brings me to a vitally important clarification relating to what you have said about reducing meat consumption. It is of course true that with a population of eight, nine, ten or 11.5 billion, the last of which is one prediction for the end of the century, we will not all be able to eat meat in the prodigious amounts currently consumed in most developed countries. But while most attention is now focused on reducing the number of ruminants on the planet due to their methane emissions, which of course do contribute to global warming, though to a much smaller extent than most people have been led to believe, it is actually only grass, the one crop we humans cannot eat, which has the capacity to restore soils to productivity by rebuilding both organic matter and structure. And the only way to get human edible food from grass is to stock it with grazing animals.

And that, I have to say, presents a problem for those who argue that if we halved the number of ruminants, agriculture would miraculously become sustainable. Sadly the exact opposite is true. Yes, we must reduce meat consumption, and in many cases stocking density, but grass also needs to be reintroduced onto prime arable land. Grass and grazing livestock are also essential for biodiversity. As such, the greatest reductions are needed in relation to animals that predominantly consume grain. This is most notably chickens, despite the fact that the birds produce only minimal amounts of methane, but also intensive pigs and grain fed beef.

Rachel Carson, of course, pointed out the damage being done to wildlife by agrochemicals, but the response of the environmental and conservation movements has been to agree to the separation of nature conservation from food production, land sparing instead of land sharing, with unrestricted use of agrochemicals on all but small pockets of land taken out of food production. Yet this approach has clearly not worked, with dramatic declines in wildlife and species diversity still continuing to occur.

This isn't to say that all cattle and sheep production is currently benign, far from it. However, if managed in the right way all pasture-based livestock production systems have the potential to be sustainable, whereas continuous arable cropping does not. In the UK, for example, a large number of birds and pollinators coexist in harmony with grazing animals and one of the many reasons for their decline is that species-rich grassland has become entirely absent from some areas, as the mono-cropping of vast areas of wheat and oilseed rape have come to predominate.

So in summary, what I'm saying is that hand in hand with the need to control population growth, in order to feed a peak world population sustainably, the reintegration of crop and livestock production in the form of more mixed farming systems will be an absolute necessity. Ideally, we should also strive to match food production and population in the UK more closely by reducing the amount of livestock feed we import and eating more of the foods we can naturally produce ourselves.

It's taken me a long time to move on from my former recalcitrant stance on organic farming and develop a broader position, without changing my fundamental beliefs. In relation to over-population it's taken a long time for my eyes to be opened to the urgent need for further action. But, if I can swallow my pride and change, as I believe I have done, then maybe we can help other, more important, figures to broaden their positions too.

30 July 2015

⇨ The above information is reprinted with kind permission from the Sustainable Food Trust. Please visit www. sustainablefoodtrust.org for further information.

© *Sustainable Food Trust 2015*

Inside India's sterilisation camps

An article from **The Conversation.**

THE CONVERSATION

By Sabu S Padmadas, Professor of Demography and Global Health, University of Southampton

A sterilisation camp held in Chhattisgarh, an impoverished state in central India, has claimed the lives of 13 women, most of whom were young and marginalised. The women, who died within hours of the procedure, were among a group of 83 patients sterilised over the course of just five hours at the mobile clinic. It now appears they died as a result of contaminated medicines. The incident raises critical questions about surgical standards, infection control protocols and post-operative care in India's reproductive health and family-planning programme.

The tragedy that unfolded at this clinic shows how urgently the approach taken to sterilisation in India needs to be changed. Warnings have been made before about conditions in these camps. In 1994, as part of a team of researchers, I observed 48 procedures carried out in just over two hours at a camp in Kerala, a state in the southern region which ranks the highest among Indian states in terms of human capital, social and health development.

"The tragedy that unfolded at this clinic shows how urgently the approach taken to sterilisation in India needs to be changed"

Yet, surprisingly, regulations were being violated at the campsite and poor hygiene standards and a lack of decent infrastructure were clear. There was inadequate counselling for the patients undergoing sterilisation and they were not getting follow-up attention.

The history of sterilisation

The debate on the quality of care in Indian family planning programmes dates back even before this time though. The Government first introduced mass sterilisation camps in the 1970s. At that time, India and China had similar fertility rates of six children per woman. The two countries took different routes in response to the problem but both were seeking long-term solutions to controlling their rapid population growth.

Female sterilisation continues to be the most popular and dominant method of contraception in India. This is especially the case in southern states, which managed to achieve a fertility below replacement level way back in the late 1980s and 1990s – so each couple had just enough children to replace them.

The programme initially promoted vasectomies and targeted couples with two or more children. The Government set targets and health providers were offered cash incentives to recruit eligible couples for sterilisation. Many men, including those who were unmarried and illiterate – or were political opponents of the Government – were coerced into accepting sterilisation without consent.

The vasectomy programme was deemed a major failure. There was serious a public backlash, blaming the Government for forcing sterilisation on poor people. Evaluations of the programme identified weaknesses including method failure, side effects and sub-standard quality of care during and after the procedure. The ruling Congress Government even had to step down during an emergency period in 1975–77, following allegations made about the coercive family planning programme.

Since the 1980s, sterilisation programmes have focused solely on women. Now, more than two-thirds of contraceptive use in India is female sterilisation. In some southern and western states, as many as 50% of women have been sterilised. The method has been widely used, mostly by young women, across India for more than three generations. In most cases, women have few options and rely directly on sterilisation as the first method of contraception they ever use. Although the Government removed family planning targets in 1998, there is still evidence of coercion in sterilisation camps in many parts of India.

"Female sterilisation continues to be the most popular and dominant method of contraception in India"

Following the rules?

There are national guidelines about how sterilisation camps should be organised, the clinical training that staff need to receive and the essential medical supplies that should be on hand – including antiseptic solutions and drugs. Sterilisation camps, in mobile or institutional settings, mostly operate at the district or sub-district level and are co-ordinated by the district health administrators. For both clients and providers, the camps are convenient, easy to access and cost-effective. Only qualified and trained medical professionals are allowed to conduct sterilisations.

Local health workers recruit women or their husbands and usually arrange transport facilities to the camps. They have to provide adequate information about the procedure to clients including potential side effects, indications and contra-indications associated with the method.

The clients are expected to declare their age, family information, medical history and physical and mental health status before the procedure. They should undergo physical and laboratory examinations prior to the surgery. The protocols require clients to make an informed, voluntary decision to be sterilised and counselling services are offered to help them make that choice.

"Undoubtedly, a long-term solution is educating and empowering women to make informed choices"

There is, however, evidence to suggest that in most camp settings, these protocols are overlooked or violated for the sake of convenience or due to high case loads. Botched sterilisation surgeries have been reported on a number of occasions in India, especially in remote and deprived areas. Level of care and negligence has remained a major concern more generally in the delivery of family planning services and particularly those requiring clinical assistance.

Challenges ahead

The Indian population is still growing at an annual rate of 1.2%. Larger states such as Uttar Pradesh, Bihar and Rajasthan are predicted to almost double in size over the next 30 years. On the other hand, young couples in India increasingly want small families. And given persistently high rates of early marriages and long exposure in the reproductive life, sterilisation

"The Indian population is still growing at an annual rate of 1.2%. Larger states such as Uttar Pradesh, Bihar and Rajasthan are predicted to almost double in size over the next 30 years"

is a highly effective method that limits the number of unwanted pregnancies and abortions. In fact, there is a high use of sterilisation among women who have just given a birth and those who have had an abortion.

Undoubtedly, a long-term solution is educating and empowering women to make informed choices.

There is a dire need for considering innovative strategies to promoting family planning information, education and counselling services – especially in rural areas where women are often forced to surrender to the state-sponsored and incentive-based family planning programmes.

Programme managers need to ensure gender balance in the promotion of contraceptive methods. That could mean revisiting vasectomy as the preferred option, since it is relatively less risky than tubectomy or laparoscopy.

With such a high demand for reproductive care, it is essential that health systems offering family planning services at various levels are systematically monitored and evaluated to ensure that quality of care standards are met. Even though these camps might be coercing some into sterilisation, there is evidently high demand for the procedure. So the standard of care on offer must be guaranteed or more women will be risking their lives.

14 November 2014

⇨ The above information is reprinted with kind permission from *The Conversation*. Please visit www.theconversation.com for further information.

© 2010–2015, The Conversation Trust (UK)

China ends one-child policy after 35 years

Government to allow all couples to have two children as "response to an ageing population" and amid concerns over economy.

By Tom Phillips

China has scrapped its one-child policy, allowing all couples to have two children for the first time since draconian family planning rules were introduced more than three decades ago.

The announcement followed a four-day Communist Party summit in Beijing where China's top leaders debated financial reforms and how to maintain growth at a time of heightened concerns about the economy.

China will "fully implement a policy of allowing each couple to have two children as an active response to an ageing population", the Party said in a statement published by Xinhua, the official news agency. "The change of policy is intended to balance population development and address the challenge of an ageing population."

Some celebrated the move as a positive step towards greater personal freedom in China. But human rights activists and critics said the loosening – which means the Communist Party continues to control the size of Chinese families – did not go far enough.

"The state has no business regulating how many children people have," said William Nee, a Hong Kong-based activist for Amnesty International.

"If China is serious about respecting human rights, the Government should immediately end such invasive and punitive controls over people's decisions to plan families and have children."

For months there has been speculation that Beijing was preparing to abandon the divisive family planning rule, which was introduced in 1980 because of fears of a population boom.

Demographers in and outside China have long warned that its low fertility rate – which experts say lies somewhere between 1.2 and 1.5 children a woman – was driving the country towards a demographic crisis.

Since 2013, there has been a gradual relaxation of China's family planning laws that already allowed minority ethnic families and rural couples whose firstborn was a girl to have more than one child.

Thursday's announcement that all couples would be allowed two children caught many experts by surprise.

"I'm shaking to be honest," said Stuart Gietel-Basten, a University of Oxford demographer who has argued for the end of the one-child policy. "It's one of those things that you have been working on and saying for years and recommending they should do something and it finally happened. It's just a bit of a shock."

The Communist Party credits the policy with preventing 400 million births, thus contributing to China's dramatic economic takeoff since the 1980s.

But the human toll has been immense, with forced sterilisations, infanticide and sex-selective abortions that have caused a dramatic gender imbalance that means millions of men will never find female partners.

"The gender imbalance is going to be a very major problem," warned Steve Tsang, a professor of contemporary Chinese studies at the University of Nottingham. "We are talking about between 20 million and 30 million young men who are not going to be able to find a wife. That creates social problems and that

Say hello to your little sister.

For 35 years **this** was illegal

creates a huge number of people who are frustrated."

History showed that countries with a very large number of unmarried men of military age were more likely to pursue aggressive, militarist foreign policy initiatives, Tsang said.

In one of the most shocking recent cases of human rights abuses related to the one-child policy, a woman who was seven months pregnant was abducted by family planning officials in Shaanxi Province in 2012 and forced to have an abortion.

Opponents say the policy has created a demographic "timebomb", with China's 1.3 billion-strong population ageing rapidly, and the country's labour pool shrinking. The UN estimates that by 2050 China will have about 440 million people over 60. The working-age population – those between 15 and 59 – fell by 3.71 million last year, a trend that is expected to continue.

There were no immediate details on how or when China's new 'two-child policy' would be implemented. But Gietel-Basten said the policy change was good news for both China's people and its leaders, who stood to gain from ending a highly unpopular rule.

"From a political, pragmatic perspective, loosening the policy is good for the Party but also it is a good thing for individual couples who want to have that second child. It is a kind of win-win for everybody," he said.

"Millions of ordinary Chinese couples will be allowed to have a second child if they want to – this is clearly a very positive thing."

Experts said the relaxation of family planning rules is unlikely to have a lasting demographic impact, particularly in urban areas where couples were now reluctant to have two children because of the high cost.

"Just because the Government says you can have another child, it doesn't mean the people will immediately follow," said Liang Zhongtang, a demographer at the Shanghai Academy of Social Science.

Gietel-Basten said: "In the short term, probably there will be a little baby boom particularly in some of the poorer provinces where the rules have been very strict, like in Sichuan or in parts of the south. But in the long term I don't think it's going to make an enormous amount of difference."

Dai Qing, a Chinese writer who has publicly called for all family planning rules to be scrapped, said the announcement was a positive step.

"It shows that the authorities have understood the changes in the total population and the demographic structure and started to address them," she said.

But Dai said questions remained, particularly about how Beijing would enforce its new two-child policy.

"Even if people are allowed to have two children, what if they want to have three children or more? What if unmarried women want to have their own children? At the end of the day, it's about women's reproductive rights and freedoms."

Others expressed concern that the announcement of the new two-child policy, which referred to Chinese couples, suggested children born outside of wedlock would continue to be penalised by the Government.

Liang called on the Communist Party to completely dismantle its unpopular and outdated family planning rules.

"I think they should abolish the family planning [system] once and for all and let people decide how many children they want to have. Only that way can they straighten out their relationship with the people."

But Gietel-Basten said it would have been virtually unthinkable for Beijing to completely abandon its family planning rules.

"That would in some ways imply that the policy was wrong... which of course would be a smack in the face of the last two generations of policymakers who stuck by it," he said.

"Getting rid of it completely probably wasn't an option in the short term. But in the long term it's certainly not inconceivable that they would move towards a pronatalist policy at some point, maybe over the next five or ten years, and that they would develop policies similar to in Korea or in Taiwan, or in Hong Kong or in Singapore, where there would be incentives for couples with one child to have a second child. I certainly think that is the future direction it [policy] is likely to go in."

As news that the notorious policy was coming to an end spread on Thursday, Chinese citizens celebrated on social media, while also lamenting how long change had taken to arrive.

Some government critics expressed their contempt for the policy by altering photographs of the red Communist Party propaganda banners that adorn towns and villages across China urging residents to obey family planning rules.

"We reward families with two children and fine those with only one," read one spoof poster mocking Beijing's change of heart. "Those who decide not to have children or who are infertile should be thrown in jail."

Additional reporting by Luna Lin.

29 October 2015

⇨ The above information is reprinted with kind permission from *The Guardian*. Please visit www.theguardian.com for further information.

As China ends the one-child policy, what is its legacy?

An article from **The Conversation.**

By Stephanie Gordon, PhD candidate, University of Leicester

THE CONVERSATION

China has announced the end to its infamous one-child policy, the restrictive rule that has limited many families to one child, and some to two children for the past 37 years. The changes will allow all couples to have two children.

China has a long history of controlling its population. Throughout the 1950s, family planning was encouraged under Mao Zedong to promote economic growth. But only in 1973 did it become a political priority, with the national wan, xi, shao – "late marriage, longer spacing, and fewer children" campaign encouraging two children per couple.

In June 1978, a policy of one child per couple was rigorously pursued as the Government feared that China would not be able to modernise and support a large population at the same time.

Yet the law was difficult to enforce. Male children were prized and families who first gave birth to a daughter would lack a son to support them in old age. From 1984 onward, responding to societal unrest, rural couples whose first child was a girl were allowed to conceive a second child.

A series of changes took place from 2010, after it emerged 13 million children were on record as being without proof of identity (*hukou*) because they were denied birth registration as a result of family planning policies.

The National Health Ministry and National Population and Family Planning Commission were merged in 2013, which signalled a relaxation of birth control as a government priority. In November 2013 the state decreed that citizens were allowed to have two children if either member of the couple was an only child themselves. The new announcement marks the most radical change of all: two children allowed for all couples.

Children with no identity

From forced abortions, sterilisation and astronomical fines, the one-child policy led to a plethora of human rights abuses.

From the beginning there were questions about how best to enforce it. One way was to charge citizens who had more than one child "social compensation fees", colloquially referred to as "fines", from two to eight times the annual incomes in rural areas, or annual disposable income in urban areas. With the income derived from these fines, livelihoods and careers of government staff depended on charging fees for unauthorised children. For example, in Henan Province alone the Population and Family Planning Commission employed 17,000 administrators and 22,000 nursing and technical staff.

In the early days, mass sterilisations and abortions were particularly rife in the early 1980s. As time went on, great pressure was put on mothers with one child to accept an IUD coil, and mothers with two children to be sterilised. In many areas children could not have their birth recorded until this took place. Mothers and families who could not afford fines for giving birth to unauthorised children would see no choice but to undergo an abortion.

When births could not be prevented, then local government could deny legal identity documentation to children born without permission. This was initially a way to hide unauthorised births. In this way, the child did not exist on government records or population statistics. Even the parents themselves might prefer to lose out on their child's *hukou* than be punished for an unauthorised child.

Over time, as China's birth rate decelerated and the population aged, local governments worried less about fulfilling birthing targets. Later on, denial of the hukou would be used as leverage

to enforce payments of fines. Without it, parents would face their child being barred from obtaining an education and being unable to obtain an ID card, or paying the outstanding fines. Assets could be seized, bank accounts frozen, or a parent detained for 15 days at a time and taken to court when parents refused to pay up.

The legacy of 4-2-1 families

The driving factor behind the relaxations is that control over births is no longer necessary. China's population is ageing rapidly. Longer life expectancy means that by 2050 it is expected that for every 100 people aged 20-64, there will be 45 people aged over 65. This has led to the "4-2-1" family where a child of working age could have to care for two parents and four grandparents in retirement.

Equally troubling is China's skewed gender ratio. In 2014, China now has 33 million more men than women – believed to be a consequence of selective abortion and female child abandonment exacerbated by family planning restrictions. Without radical changes, many men (usually referred to as "bare sticks") will be unable to find wives.

Some will question if China's abandonment of its one-child policy will really lead to more births, as the previous relaxation in 2013 did little to boost birth rates. Others will note that the policy is not really over: couples are still limited to two children. Meanwhile, with giving birth out of wedlock still effectively illegal, some will question if the relaxations go far enough.

29 October 2015

⇨ The above information is reprinted with kind permission from *The Conversation*. Please visit www.theconversation.com for further information.

Only child guilt? Five reasons it's cool to stop at one

By Georgia James

The British family is shrinking, with almost half (46%) of families in England and Wales having just one child, according to the most recent ONS figures.

And it's predicted that by the end of the decade these single-child families will be in the majority.

Fuelled by financial constraints – economic uncertainty, soaring house prices and exorbitant childcare costs – and lifestyle choices, such as later parenthood and an increasing number of women juggling family with careers, the only child has never been less 'alone'.

Yet the stigma surrounding so-called 'onlies' – and their parents – is still rife.

"I feel that I have constantly been viewed by mums with more than one child as an inexperienced, ill-qualified, mummy-lite," writes Parentdish writer and mother of one, Kelly Rose Bradford.

"Now my 'baby' is nine and I am 39, this has morphed more into wet-eyed, pitying glances, tight smiles and 'bet you really wish you'd had more while you could' low-voiced sympathies," she adds.

The view that only children fall into two stereotypes – the 'maladjusted loner, lacking in social skills' and the 'egocentric, spoilt brat' – goes hand in hand with the notion that parents actively choosing to have one child are selfish for depriving their child of siblings.

And this stereotyping only exacerbates the anguish of the many parents who are unable to have a second or third child due to age, fertility or relationship factors.

Nobody is disputing the benefits of siblings. Aside from rivalries and the complex dynamics of birth order, two-or-three children families have long since been viewed as the ideal dynamic.

But with single child families rapidly replacing 2.4 children as the societal norm, we decided it was time to debunk the myths surrounding 'lonely onlies', challenge the stigma pinned on their 'selfish' parents and look at the positive sides of the downsized family unit.

A quick call-out to find only children, and the parents of onlies, willing to share their positive stories for this feature, made one thing abundantly clear: missing out on siblings need not mean missing out on life.

MYTH: only children are spoiled

"I wasn't spoiled," says Dan, 42, an only child with one daughter, Daisy, two. "I don't think being an only child had much influence on how I turned out. The relationship with the parents is by far the biggest influencing factor."

Sarah, 38, from Cardiff, agrees: "If there is one division of parents dead-set on ensuring their children are not spoiled, it's those of only children," she says.

"My parents went to great lengths to make sure I didn't have life handed to me on a plate. Pocket money and new toys were earned in exchange for help around the house, so I never took things for granted."

And having siblings doesn't automatically exempt you from the 'spoiled' category, points out Ash, 25, from Bristol: "I've never behaved like that, but I know plenty of people who grew up with hordes of brothers and sisters who are among the most self-centred people I know."

"I'm really close to my parents – they're always the first people I turn to in a crisis, even if I know what they're going to tell me is what I don't always want to hear"

MYTH: only children are lonely

Mixing with peers is an essential part of a child's development. But nurseries, after-school clubs, neighbouring families and the plethora of local child-friendly activities now available to youngsters, mean socialising is no longer restricted to the confines of the family home.

"Somehow even the title 'only child' has a ring of sadness about it – some suggestion there must be something for such a child to overcome," says David, who lives with his partner and three-year-old son, Louis, in Reykjavik.

"Somehow even the title 'only child' has a ring of sadness about it – some suggestion there must be something for such a child to overcome"

"We have many good friends who live literally minutes walk away who have kids Louis's age, as well as both older and younger. He is very used to not being the only child around, and to socialising with kids of other ages."

"Besides, being alone doesn't necessarily equate to being lonely," says Jenny, 40, an only child with one seven-year-old daughter, Sophie. "I've always liked my own company, which I think has made me very self-sufficient and self-motivated."

She adds: "There's this idea of a gaping void in the life of an only child. But Sophie has never expressed an interest in having a sibling. She has plenty of friends – and having a dog helps!"

"I am an only child and I've never felt that I've missed out on having siblings. I make my family out of friends," says Suzie, 35.

"My son has plenty of friends at preschool and I make sure he has lots of opportunities to play with them. I'm sure it's lovely if you have a close relationship with a sibling, but there's absolutely no guarantee that you would get on with them," she adds.

MYTH: parents who choose to have one child are selfish

"Selfish is a word that comes up over and over again when it comes to only children. But being selfish can be a good thing," explains Jenny.

"Endless compromise does no one any favours and a few of my friends have the wrecked relationships to prove it."

Tom, 29, from Sheffield, agrees:

The way I see it, happy and relaxed parents equal a happy and relaxed child.

"Having more holidays, more money, more space at home and more time for each other as a couple, as well as a family, are not just perks for my wife and me. All of these things will give our son Lucas a better quality of life, too.

"I feel that as long as I make sure that I'm Eloise's friend and companion as well as her mummy, and that her family friends are lifelong, she won't miss a sibling"

"As long as we ensure he gets plenty of opportunity to make strong and lasting friendships I don't think we are depriving him in any way."

A close parental bond

Being stuck with 'the olds' might sound boring to those with siblings, but only children can have a unique closeness with their parents.

"I'm really close to my parents – they're always the first people I turn to in a crisis, even if I know what they're going to tell me is what I don't always want to hear," says Ash.

"I believe that my strong bond comes because I always had their undivided attention – I never had to turn to other people growing up, as friends of mine often had to because they had a wayward brother or sister who was taking up a lot of their parents' time."

Households by size, United Kingdom, 2011–2014				
Number of households	2011 estimate	2012 estimate	2013 estimate	2014 estimate
One person	7,660	7,717	7,752	7,586
Two people	9,246	9,286	9,152	9,342
Three people	4,255	4,367	4,367	4,311
Four people	3,530	3,555	3,638	3,708
Five people	1,169	1,165	1,211	1,208
Six or more people	548	524	533	548
Source: Labour Force Survey (LFS), *Office for National Statistics*				

Speech bubble: "OKAY – PICK THE ONLY CHILD..."

Lucy, 42, mother to Eloise, three, believes adapting the way you raise your child according to the dynamic, counteracts the potential issues facing only children: "I feel that as long as I make sure that I'm Eloise's friend and companion as well as her mummy, and that her family friends are lifelong, she won't miss a sibling."

"it's hardly surprising money is a major driver behind Britain's shrinking family"

But can a close relationship have its drawbacks?

"Being hyper-critical, I could say our son gets spoiled with our love – there's no sibling to make him question anything in this area," says Suzie.

"But is that bad? To have such a secure base to develop self-esteem from? I've absolutely no doubt that parents of more than one child love them equally, but it's got to be difficult for niggling insecurities about divided loyalty not to crop up at some point."

Less financial pressure

Parents spend £9,610 a year feeding, clothing and educating each new member of the family, according to a 2010 report. This makes the average cost of raising a child to the age of 21, a whopping £201,809. And that doesn't include uniforms, sports equipment and school trips, which add a further £52,881.

That's almost a quarter of a million pounds in all. So, it's hardly surprising money is a major driver behind Britain's shrinking family.

"I freelance, and can't work for a month in the summer when Louis' playschool is closed. I am also the one who takes care of him when he's sick as I can be more flexible with my time. I nevertheless earn less as a result," says David.

"How can we expect to earn more money to pay for the additional expense of a second child? Work harder? Longer hours? More exhaustion, stress and less time with this wonderful boy?"

"Being hyper-critical, I could say our son gets spoiled with our love – there's no sibling to make him question anything in this area"

Suzie agrees that reducing financial stress can have a big impact on family life. "We have no intention of spoiling Xander, materially," says Suzie. "But it's nice to know it will be easier to provide for him – not to mention, much cheaper to organise childcare." Holidays would be thin on the ground if we had two," says Jenny. "And then we'd have to find a bigger place to live... and the list goes on."

If the anecdotal evidence of a few happy, single-child families isn't enough to convince you, there is a growing raft of research to support the case for only children, too.

Toni Falbo, Professor of Educational Psychology at the University of Texas' Population Research Center, who has studied the outcomes of only children in the US and China for more than 30 years, says, if anything only children have an advantage when it comes to self-esteem, motivation and academic achievement.

And research undertaken at Ohio State University also revealed that being an only child does not make youngsters lonely, unable to make friends, spoiled or selfish.

14 August 2014

⇨ The above information is reprinted with kind permission from The Huffington Post UK. Please visit www.huffingtonpost.co.uk for further information.

Key facts

- The population trends projected by the UN vary enormously by region:

  - Africa and much of Asia are predicted to grow significantly;

  - the Americas are expected to grow somewhat; and

  - Europe is predicted to stabilise. (page 1)

- The mid-range global projection is that the planet's population will increase from seven billion to nine billion by 2050. Broader estimates range from eight to 11 billion. (page 1)

- The population of the UK at 30 June 2014 is estimated to be 64,596,800. (page 2)

- Over the year to mid-2014 the number of people resident in the UK increased by 491,100 (up 0.77%), which is above the average annual increase (0.75%) seen over the last decade. (page 2)

- The population of the UK almost reached 64.6 million in mid-2014 with the total UK population standing at 64,596,800. (page 3)

- There are presently 391 local authorities in the UK; 326 in England, 32 in Scotland, 22 in Wales and 11 in Northern Ireland. In mid-2014, the local authority with the smallest population size at 2,300 was Isles of Scilly and the largest population at 1,101,400 was Birmingham. (page 4)

- The UK population grew to an estimated 64.6 million in 2014, its highest ever value. This represents an increase of almost half a million people from 2013 according to the most recent population estimates. (page 5)

- Natural change has resulted in increases in the population in every year over the last decade, by around 200,000 people per year on average over the previous decade and in 2014 it increased the UK population by more than 200,000 people. (page 5)

- Germany and France are the only two EU countries with bigger populations than the UK's, but they had lower growth rates at five and 4.5 per 1,000. (page 7)

- "Life expectancy is rising faster than thought, with 90 expected to become the norm in some affluent areas of the country by 2030," The Guardian reports. (page 8)

- Life expectancy in England and Wales is expected to continue to rise from the 2012 average of 79.5 years for men and 83.3 for women, to 85.7 (95% credible interval 84.2 to 87.4) for men and 87.6 (95% credible interval 86.7 to 88.9) for women by 2030. (page 9)

- By 2025, world population could be more than eight billion people. Around 2047 it could hit nine billion and by 2100 it could reach 11 billion – although there is still much uncertainty around this number with some estimates reaching 16 billion. (page 10)

- More than half (54%) of the increase of the UK population between 1991 and 2012 was due to the direct contribution of net migration. (page 11)

- In 1996, when the population of England was 49 million, it was projected to be around 51 million today. The latest figures from the Office for National Statistics show that it now stands at just over 54 million. (page 13)

- Overall, the global population growth rate is projected to fall to 0.5 per cent per annum by 2050. (page 17)

- Out of 233 countries or areas, 191 (82 per cent) experienced increases in the proportion of older persons between 1980 and 2015. 231 countries or areas (99 per cent) are expected to see an increase in the proportion aged 60 or over between 2015 and 2050. (page 18)

- 225 million women in developing countries who want to plan their families and their lives have unmet need for contraception. (page 20)

- By 2050, it is expected that nearly 70% of the world's population will live in urban areas. (page 24)

- Female sterilisation continues to be the most popular and dominant method of contraception in India. (page 32)

- The Indian population is still growing at an annual rate of 1.2%. Larger states such as Uttar Pradesh, Bihar and Rajasthan are predicted to almost double in size over the next 30 years. (page 33)

- China has scrapped its one-child policy, allowing all couples to have two children for the first time since draconian family planning rules were introduced more than three decades ago. (page 34)

- The British family is shrinking, with almost half (46%) of families in England and Wales having just one child, according to the most recent ONS figures. (page 37)

Ageing population

A population whose average age is rising. This can be caused by increased life expectancy, for example following significant medical advances, or by falling birth rates, for example due to the introduction of contraception. However, the higher the proportion of older people within a population, the lower the birth rate will become due to there being fewer people of childbearing age.

Asylum seeker

Someone who has fled their country because they personally are at risk of political violence or persecution, and seek the protection of another state.

Birth rate

The number of live births within a population over a given period of time, often expressed as the number of births per 1,000 of the population.

Death rate

The number of deaths within a population over a given period of time, often expressed as number of deaths per 1,000 of the population.

Demographic changes

Demographics refer to the structure of a population. We are currently experiencing an increase in our ageing population. People are living longer thanks to advancements in medical treatment and care. Soon, the world will have more older people than children. This means that the need for long-term care is rising.

Demographics

Statistical characteristics of a population: for example, age, race or employment status.

Emigration

Leaving one's native country to live in another state. People emigrate for many reasons, but most often with the aim of seeking out better living and working conditions.

Immigrant

To immigrate is to move permanently from your home country, and settle somewhere else.

Infant mortality rate

The number of infant deaths (infants are usually defined as one year old or younger) per 1,000 live births of the population.

Long-term international migrant

A long-term international migrant is defined as someone who moves to a country other than that of his or her usual residence for a period of at least a year, so that the country of destination becomes his or her new country of usual residence.

Migration

To migrate is to move from one's home country and settle in another.

Natural change

Natural change is the number of births minus the number of deaths.

Net migration

Net migration is the number of immigrants minus the number of emigrants.

Population growth

An increase in the number of people who inhabit a specific region. This is caused by a higher birth rate and net immigration than the death rate and net emigration. Since the start of the 20th century the rate of global population growth has increased drastically, growing from just 1.6 billion at the turn of the 20th century to seven billion today.

Refugee

A person who has left their home country and cannot return because they fear that they will be persecuted on the grounds of race, religion, nationality, political affiliation or social group. In the UK a person is officially known as a refugee when they claim asylum and this claim is accepted by the Government.

Sustainable population

A population which has enough natural resources within its environment to thrive, but uses them in a manner which allows for them to be constantly renewed and replaced, thereby ensuring that resources will be available to future generations.

Assignments

Brainstorming

⇨ In small groups, discuss what you know about population. Consider the following points:

- Is the population in the UK growing?

- What factors contribute to population growth?

- Is population growth a good thing or a bad thing?

- What is happening to the global population?

Research

⇨ Create a questionnaire to find out how many children are in the families connected to your year group. You should ask each person how many siblings they have, how many siblings their parents have/had and how many siblings their grandparents have/had. Summarise your findings and create graphs to illustrate the information.

⇨ Research China's decision to change their one-child policy. Write some notes about the old laws and new laws and why they were changed.

⇨ Choose a country in Europe and research their population. Compare with a classmate.

⇨ Why might population forecasts sometimes be inaccurate? How are they calculated? Do some research to find out and then discuss with a partner and share your thoughts with the rest of your class.

Design

⇨ Design a poster that celebrates the law in China being changed to allow two children per family.

⇨ Choose one of the articles in this book and create an illustration to highlight the key themes/message of your chosen article.

⇨ What might future cities look like if the population continues to grow? In pairs or small groups, think of an invention that might help cities to house more people and maximise the use of space. Draw and annotate your invention.

⇨ Create an illustrated timeline to display the world's population growth from the beginning of the 1900s to the present day. Include any events from history which would have had an impact on population size: for example, the 'Black Death' and the discovery of penicillin. Your timeline should be historically accurate as well as visually appealing.

Oral

⇨ "The UK doesn't have room for any more people." Debate this motion as a class, with one group arguing in favour and the other against.

⇨ As a class, discuss why you think the UK population is ageing. Why are people living longer? Is this a good thing or a bad thing?

⇨ In pairs, discuss how lack of contraception in developing countries is linked to population growth and sustainability.

⇨ Research the current global population and projections for future population growth. Create a PowerPoint presentation that explores the numbers.

⇨ Read Can the Earth feed 11 billion people? on page 25 and discuss the author's point of view.

⇨ Choose one of the illustrations from this book and, with a partner, discuss why the artist chose to portray the article in the way they did.

Reading/writing

⇨ Write an article exploring life expectancy in the UK. Read the article on page eight for help.

⇨ Write a one-paragraph definition of migration.

⇨ Write a blog post from the point of view of a child with no siblings. Write about the good and bad aspects of being an only child.

⇨ Imagine you work for a charity that believes reducing the amount of children people have will help to save the planet. Write a mission statement explaining why your charity holds this belief, and then create a leaflet with further information about global population growth and its impact on sustainability.

⇨ Read the articles in chapter one and write a summary of the trends in population in the UK.

⇨ Write a letter to your student newspaper arguing that the pressure on the planet is not from rapid population growth, but from over-consumption of natural resources. You will need to support your argument with evidence, informing readers of how lifestyles in developed countries demand over-use of natural resources. You could also consider reading the Issues book Vol.290 Sustainability for further information.

Acknowledgements

The publisher is grateful for permission to reproduce the material in this book. While every care has been taken to trace and acknowledge copyright, the publisher tenders its apology for any accidental infringement or where copyright has proved untraceable. The publisher would be pleased to come to a suitable arrangement in any such case with the rightful owner.

Images

All images courtesy of iStock, except page 4 © Sonia Langford, page 10 © Michael Ash, page 12 © Anna Dziubinska, page 13 © Dwayne Paisley-Marshall and 36 © Tony Bertolino.

Icons on page 41 are courtesy of Freepik.

Illustrations

Don Hatcher: pages 1 & 24. Simon Kneebone: pages 2 & 39. Angelo Madrid: pages 14 & 34.

Additional acknowledgements

Editorial on behalf of Independence Educational Publishers by Cara Acred.

With thanks to the Independence team: Mary Chapman, Sandra Dennis, Christina Hughes, Jackie Staines and Jan Sunderland.

Cara Acred

Cambridge

January 2016